CW01650209

Keep … en
you a … in
the lc

Whether you are in your car or on foot, you will enjoy an evocative journey back in time. Compare the Dorset of old with what you can see today—see how the streets of the towns and their parks and open spaces have changed; examine the shops and buildings and notice how they have been altered or replaced; look at fine details such as lamp-posts, shop fascias and trade signs; and see the many alterations to Dorset's villages that have taken place unnoticed during our lives, some of which we may have taken for granted.

At the turn of a page you will gain fascinating insights into Dorset's unique history.

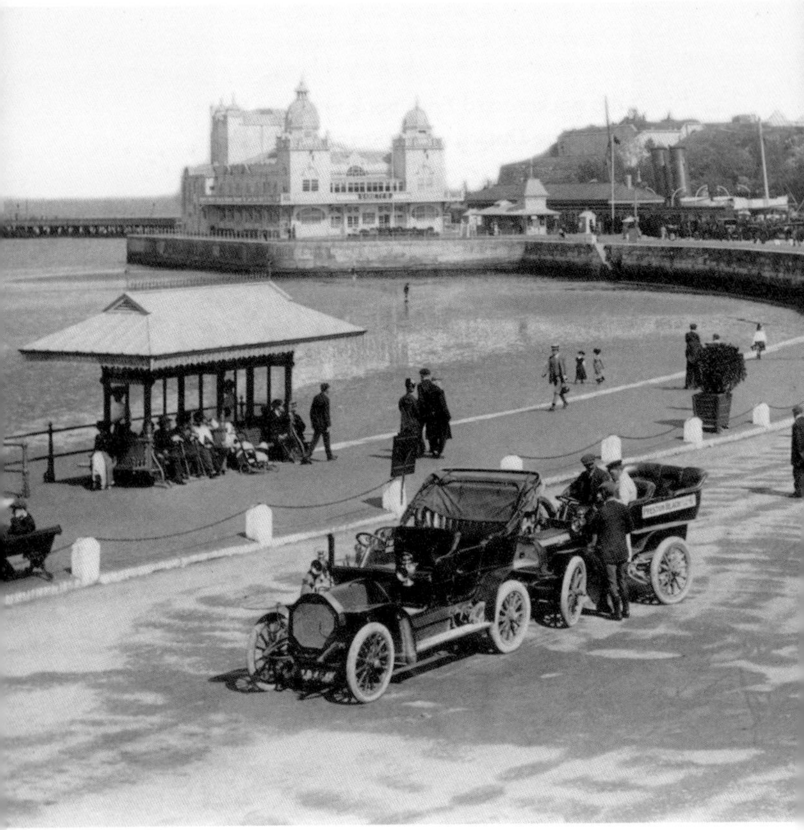

FRANCIS FRITH'S

pocket ALBUM

DORSET

A POCKET ALBUM

Adapted from an original book by
JOHN BAINBRIDGE

First published in the United Kingdom in 2006 by
The Francis Frith Collection®

ISBN 1-84589-109-0
Text and Design copyright The Francis Frith Collection®
Photographs copyright The Francis Frith Collection®
except where indicated.

The Frith® photographs and the Frith® logo are reproduced under licence from Heritage Photographic Resources Ltd, the owners of the Frith® archive and trademarks. 'The Francis Frith Collection', 'Francis Frith' and 'Frith' are registered trademarks of Heritage Photographic Resources Ltd.

All rights reserved. No photograph in this publication may be sold to a third party other than in the original form of this publication, or framed for sale to a third party. No parts of this publication may be reproduced, stored in a retrieval system, or transmitted, in any form, or by any means, electronic, mechanical, photocopying, recording or otherwise, without the prior permission of the publishers and copyright holder.

British Library Cataloguing in Publication Data

Dorset - A Pocket Album
Adapted from an original book by John Bainbridge

The Francis Frith Collection
Frith's Barn, Teffont,
Salisbury, Wiltshire SP3 5QP
Tel: +44 (0) 1722 716 376
Email: info@francisfrith.co.uk
www.francisfrith.com

Printed and bound in England.

Front Cover: DORCHESTER, HIGH WEST STREET 1930 83391t
The colour-tinting is for illustrative purposes only, and is not intended to be historically accurate.

Frontispiece: Weymouth, The Pier and the Pavilion 1909 / 61589

AS WITH ANY HISTORICAL DATABASE THE FRITH ARCHIVE IS CONSTANTLY BEING CORRECTED AND IMPROVED AND THE PUBLISHERS WOULD WELCOME INFORMATION ON OMISSIONS OR INACCURACIES

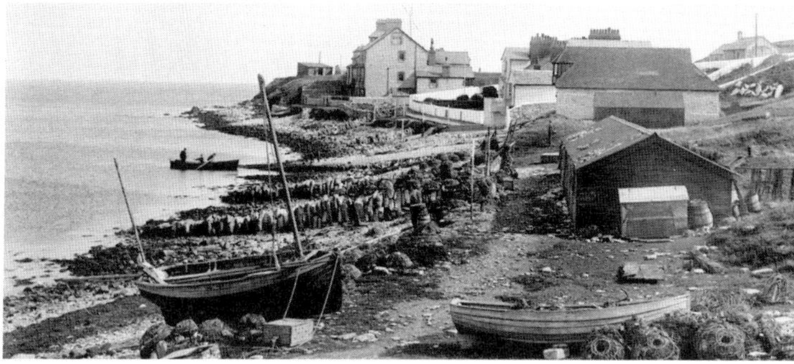

SWANAGE, THE COASTGUARD STATION 1897 / 40310

CONTENTS

4 FRANCIS FRITH: VICTORIAN PIONEER

6 DORSET - AN INTRODUCTION

9 THE INLAND TOWNS

29 THE RURAL HEARTLAND

68 ALONG THE COAST

122 INDEX

125 FREE MOUNTED PRINT VOUCHER

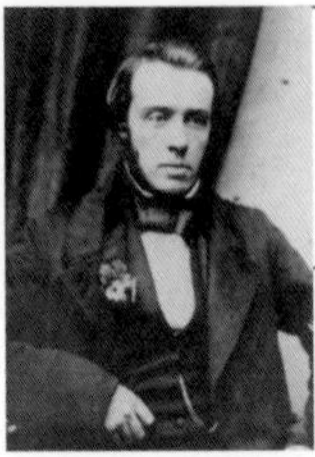

FRANCIS FRITH

VICTORIAN PIONEER

Francis Frith, founder of the world-famous photographic archive, was a complex and multi-talented man. A devout Quaker and a highly successful Victorian businessman, he was philosophic by nature and pioneering in outlook. By 1855 he had already established a wholesale grocery business in Liverpool, and sold it for the astonishing sum of £200,000, which is the equivalent today of over £15,000,000.Now in his thirties, and captivated by the new science of photography, Frith set out on a series of pioneering journeys up the Nile and to the Near East.

INTRIGUE AND EXPLORATION

He was the first photographer to venture beyond the sixth cataract of the Nile. Africa was still the mysterious 'Dark Continent', and Stanley and Livingstone's historic meeting was a decade into the future. The conditions for picture taking confound belief. He laboured for hours in his wicker dark-room in the sweltering heat of the desert, while the volatile chemicals fizzed dangerously in their trays. Back in London he exhibited his photographs and was 'rapturously cheered' by members of the Royal Society. His reputation as a photographer was made overnight.

VENTURE OF A LIFE-TIME

By the 1870s the railways had threaded their way across the country, and Bank Holidays and half-day Saturdays had been made obligatory by Act of Parliament. All of a sudden the working man and his family were able to enjoy days out, take holidays, and see a little more of the world.

With typical business acumen, Francis Frith foresaw that these new tourists would enjoy having souvenirs to commemorate their days out. For the next thirty years he travelled the country by train and by pony and trap, producing fine photographs of seaside resorts and beauty spots that were keenly bought by millions of Victorians. These prints were painstakingly pasted into family albums and pored over during the dark nights of winter, rekindling precious memories of summer excursions. Frith's studio was soon supplying retail shops all over the country, and by 1890 F Frith & Co had become the greatest specialist photographic publishing company in the world, with over 2,000 sales outlets, and pioneered the picture postcard.

FRANCIS FRITH'S LEGACY

Francis Frith had died in 1898 at his villa in Cannes, his great project still growing. The archive he created continued in business for another seventy years. By 1970 it contained over a third of a million pictures showing 7,000 British towns and villages.

Frith's legacy to us today is of immense significance and value, for the magnificent archive of evocative photographs he created provides a unique record of change in the cities, towns and villages throughout Britain over a century and more. Frith and his fellow studio photographers revisited locations many times down the years to update their views, compiling for us an enthralling and colourful pageant of British life and character.

We are fortunate that Frith was dedicated to recording the minutiae of everyday life. For it is this sheer wealth of visual data, the painstaking chronicle of changes in dress, transport, street layouts, buildings, housing, engineering and landscape that captivates us so much today, offering us a powerful link with the past and with the lives of our ancestors.

Computers have now made it possible for Frith's many thousands of images to be accessed almost instantly. The archive offers every one of us an opportunity to examine the places where we and our families have lived and worked down the years. Its images, depicting our shared past, are now bringing pleasure and enlightenment to millions around the world a century and more after his death.

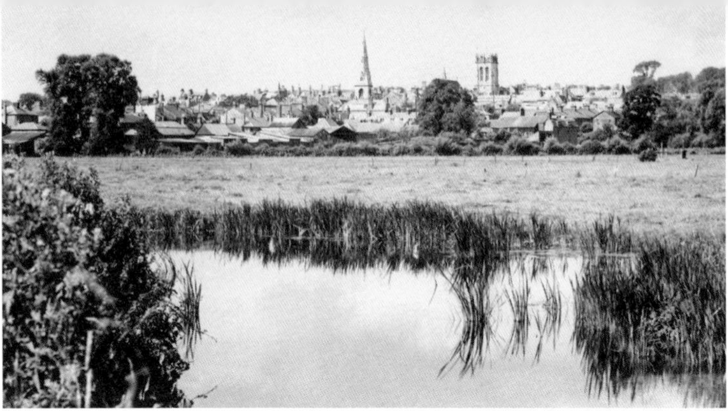

DORCHESTER, FROM THE RIVER FROME 1930 / 83388

DORSET
AN INTRODUCTION

DORSET is a county of contrasts, but with an identity all its own. Few visitors fail to fall under the spell of its scenic beauty, its deep historical and literary associations, and its inherent peace and tranquillity. Despite the growth in population, the intrusion of some modern industries, and a considerable increase in traffic since Frith visited, Dorset remains unspoiled and rural. Few English counties have been quite so fortunate.

From the deep valleys and woodlands of the west, where the county slips imperceptibly into Devon, to the high chalk downlands with their ancient ridge paths, where it is still possible to wander for much of the day with only sheep and farmworkers for company, to the lowland heaths where rare birds and butterflies crouch in the heather and gorse, this land is as English as anyone could imagine.

Many of the villages could have come straight from a picture on a box of biscuits: it is as though someone with the eye of an artist had made them with great care and purpose. Rarely do the constructions of man complement the hand of nature quite so well.

Dorset is bounded to the south by a long coastline of exquisite beauty and variety. To walk along the Dorset Coast Path, part of the longer South West Way, from the fossil cliffs of Lyme Regis to the vast expanse of Poole Harbour, would be an excellent introduction to Dorset for anyone unfamiliar with the district.

Pick any Dorset town and it is not hard to find traces of English history. Many of these settlements were here when this land was an outpost of the Roman Empire. Saxon kings endowed their religious buildings, and some lie buried in the churches they cherished. History is everywhere, only waiting to be discovered and interpreted.

Where change has occurred since the photographs in this book were taken, it has not been dramatic. Add a little more traffic and a few altered shop signs and the view is essentially the same. Away from the larger towns there has scarcely been any change at all, and it is possible to compare the scenes directly. All who love Dorset welcome this sense of permanency. Long may the county remain unchanged!

The wise visitor will stroll around Dorset's towns either in the first light of morning or the quiet of evening. Then, motor traffic is at its minimum, and it is possible to see the towns as the Frith photographer would have done. Only then can you appreciate the joys of their diverse architecture, their historical and literary associations and, above all, their sheer Englishness.

Most were settlements when the Romans held power, but the layout of many is pure Saxon. For this was the heartland of the old kingdom of Wessex, and towns such as Shaftesbury, Sherborne and Wareham still hold echoes of those powerful Saxon kings—Ethelred, Ethelbald, Ethelbert and Alfred—some of whom are buried in the honey-coloured stone churches, abbeys and minsters of the locality.

For fans of Thomas Hardy, Dorchester is for ever Casterbridge, capital of the Wessex of his marvellous novels. There is probably no better way of exploring its streets than with a copy of 'The Mayor of Casterbridge', following in the steps of Hardy's sad hero Michael Henchard. Such a stroll will reveal many of Dorchester's odd and delightful corners. This tour should be supplemented by a visit to the local museum, where Hardy's study has been meticulously recreated.

Bridport, Blandford and Wimborne long thrived as market towns, commercial centres for the villages and farmlands of a wider, unspoiled countryside. Each had their own industries. At Bridport, for instance, ropemaking provided for the local economy when the town failed as a port. Such trades were important when alternative work, such as agriculture and fishing, were so dependent on the vagaries of weather, supply failure and general unemployment.

All of these towns have a close relationship with their surrounding countryside; the fields, woods and downlands are seldom more than a half-hour's walk from their centres. To some extent, the green mantle of the Dorset countryside has shaped their development as much as the hand of man.

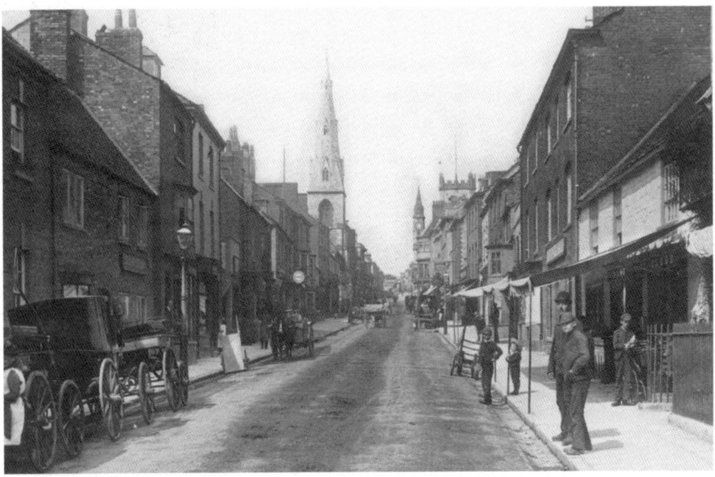

DORCHESTER, HIGH EAST STREET 1891 / 28512

DORCHESTER

HIGH WEST STREET 1891 / 28515

A walk down High West Street from Thomas Hardy's statue will bring the visitor to the County Museum, where the novelist's study has been faithfully recreated, complete with the pens used to write each novel.

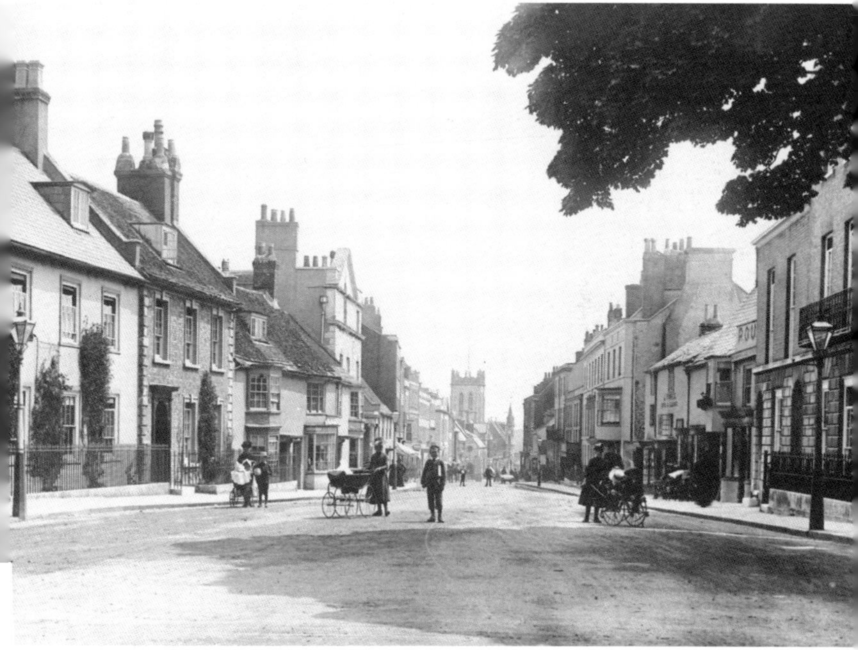

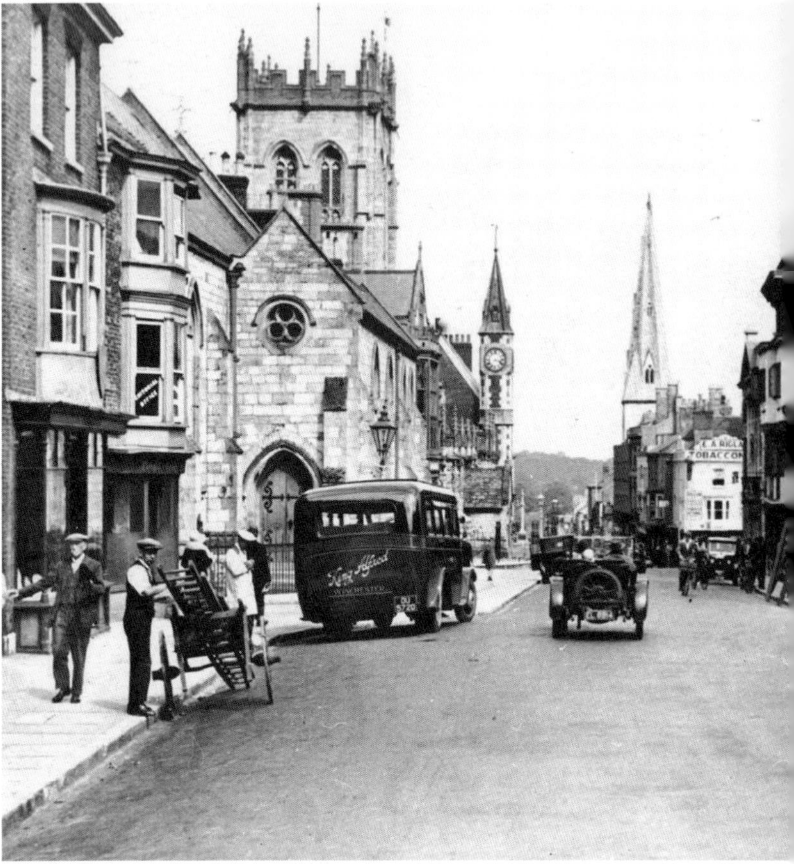

DORCHESTER

HIGH WEST STREET 1930 / 83391

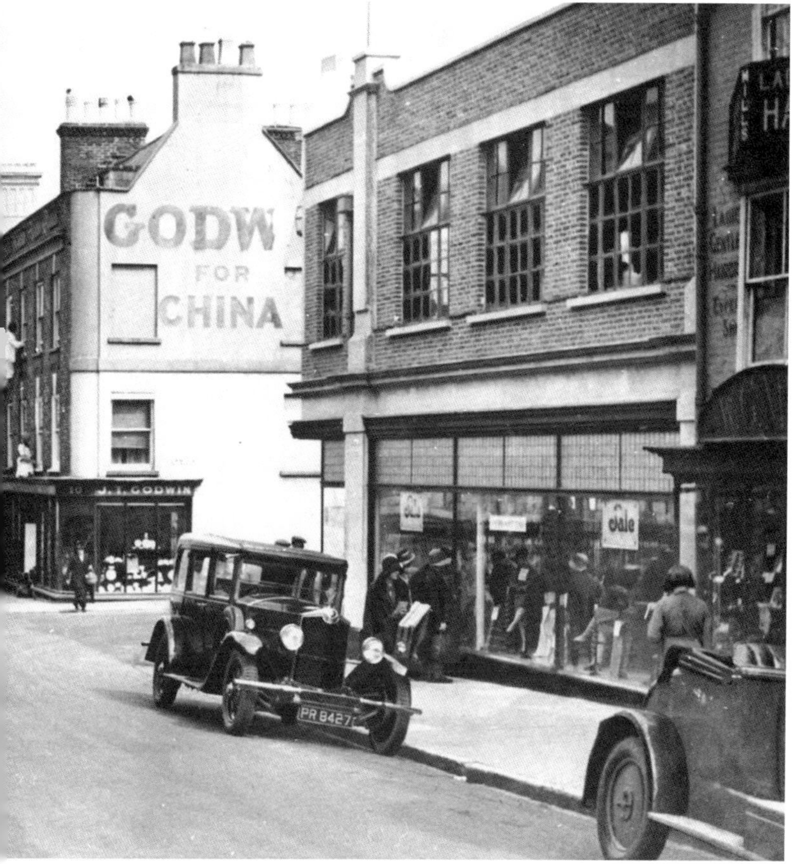

The tower of the medieval St Peter's Church, seen here on the left, dominates much of Dorchester's High Street. The building was restored in 1856 by the local architect John Hicks, with the help of his teenage apprentice Thomas Hardy. The interior is dominated by the tomb of Denzil, Lord Holles who fought for parliament in the Civil War, but survived to become a counsellor to Charles II.

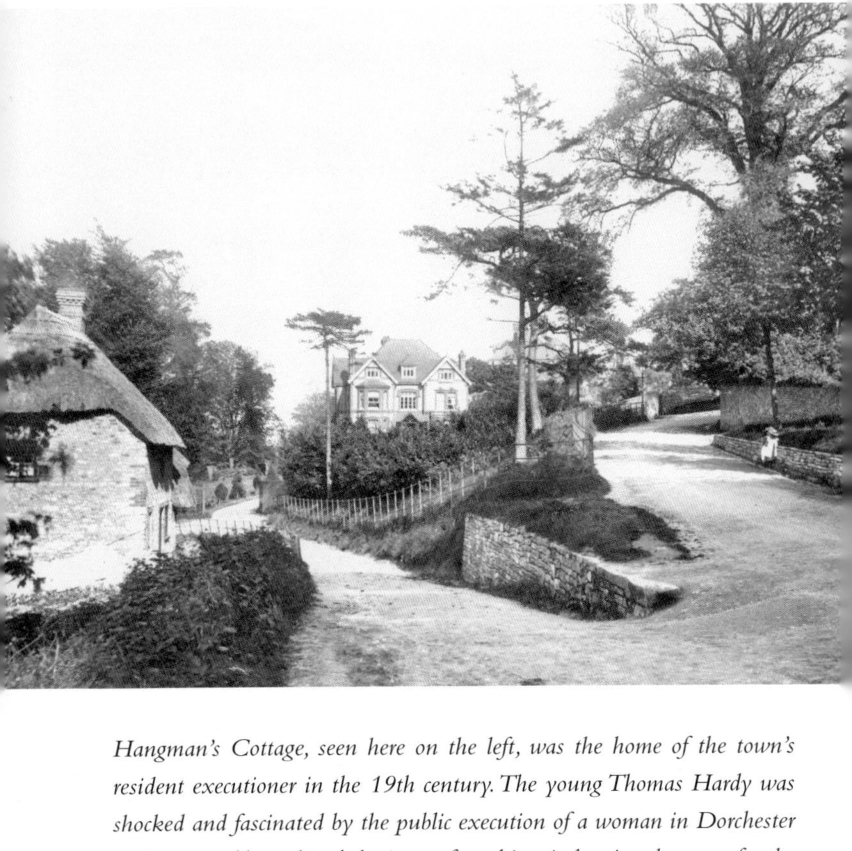

Hangman's Cottage, seen here on the left, was the home of the town's resident executioner in the 19th century. The young Thomas Hardy was shocked and fascinated by the public execution of a woman in Dorchester and was unable to dispel the image from his mind, using the scene for the climax of 'Tess of the D'Urbervilles'.

DORCHESTER

HANGMAN'S COTTAGE 1898 / 41163

Hardy designed Max Gate as his final home and wrote his greatest novels there. Many famous personalities, such as Lawrence of Arabia, came here to pay homage to the grand old man of English letters. The poet and novelist died here in 1928.

DORCHESTER

THOMAS HARDY'S HOME 1930 / 83402

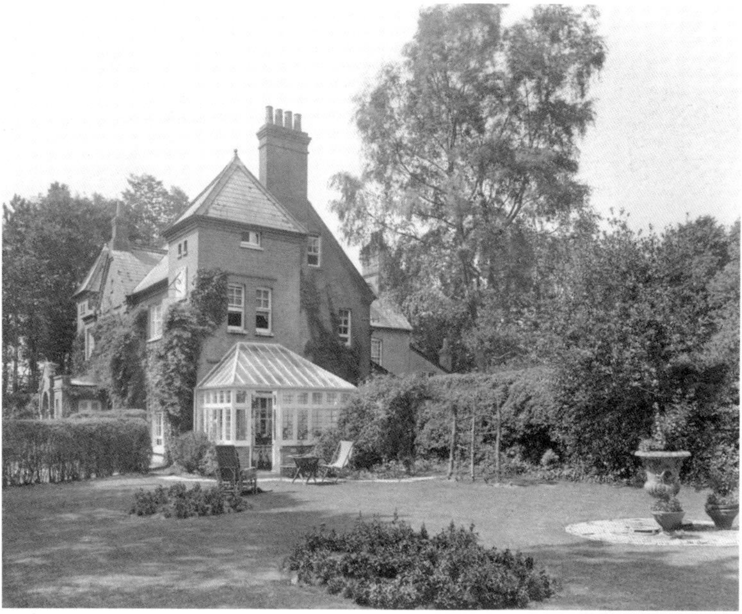

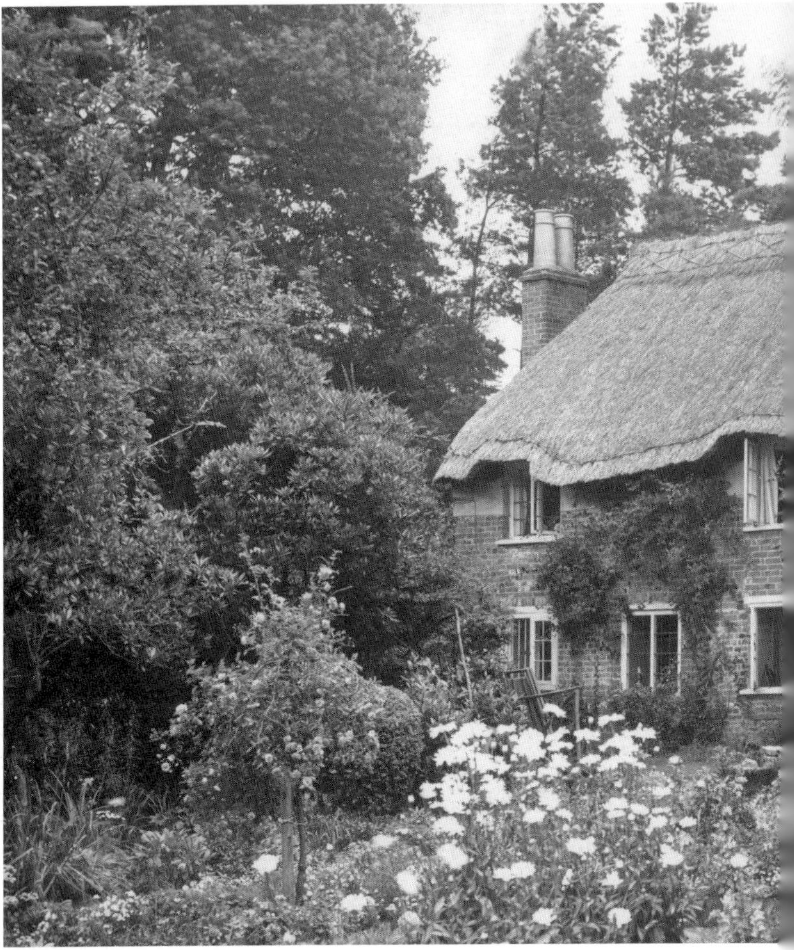

HIGHER BOCKHAMPTON

THOMAS HARDY'S BIRTHPLACE 1930 / 83400

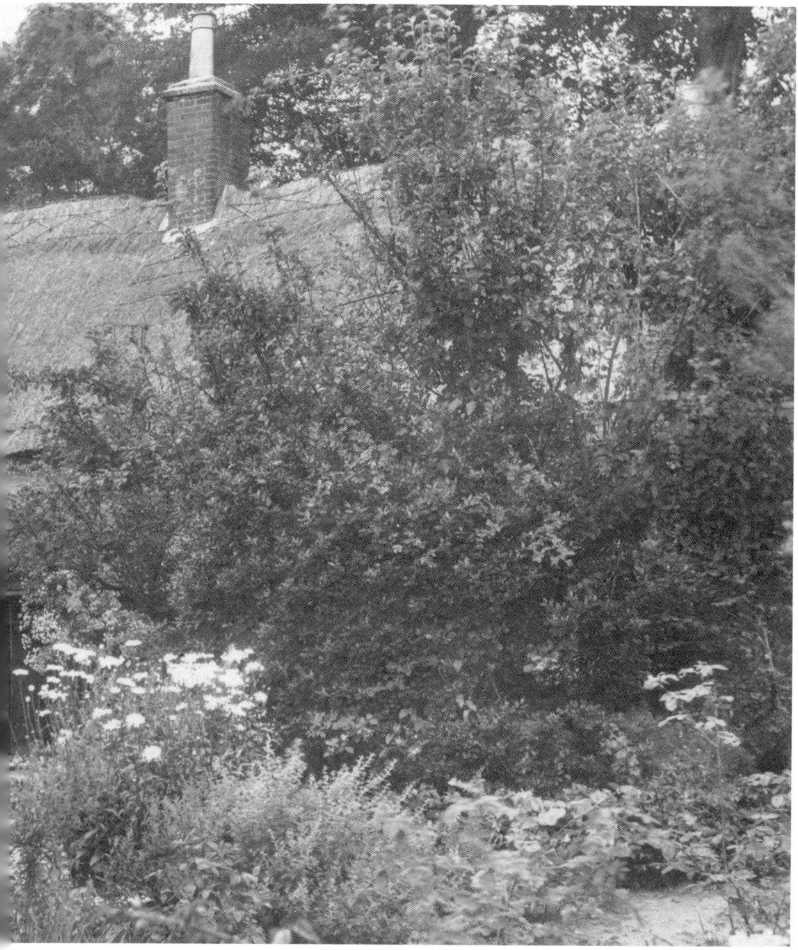

Thomas Hardy was born in this cottage in 1840 and wrote his first three novels whilst living there. He retained an interest in the family home until the end of his life. The National Trust acquired the house and surroundings in 1948, and it is regularly open to the public.

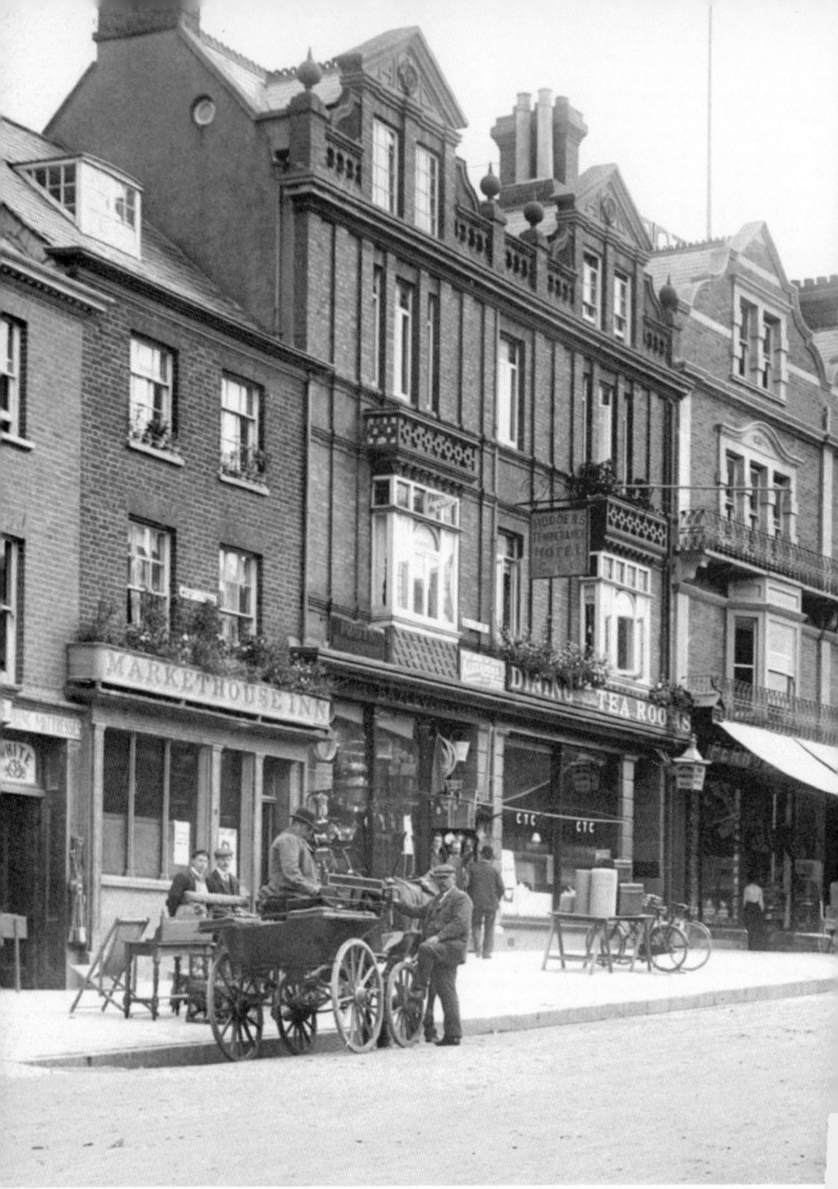
MARKETHOUSE INN
CTC
CTC

BRIDPORT

EAST STREET 1904 / 52756

The wide main streets of Bridport were originally designed to be highways, market venues and workshops. Rope and net making were considerable industries in previous centuries and the width of the thoroughfares facilitated their manufacture.

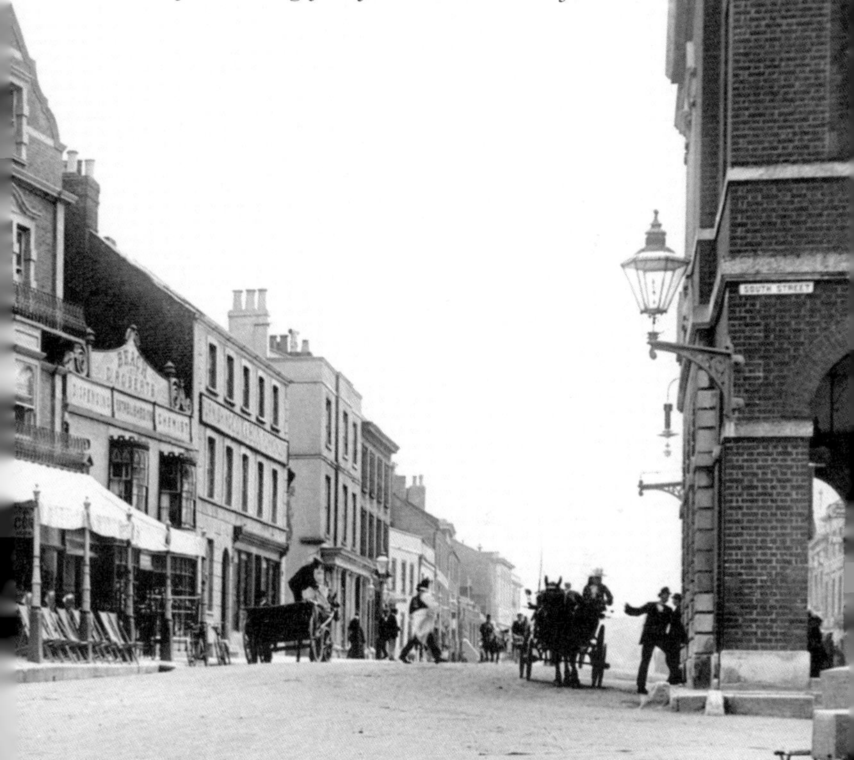

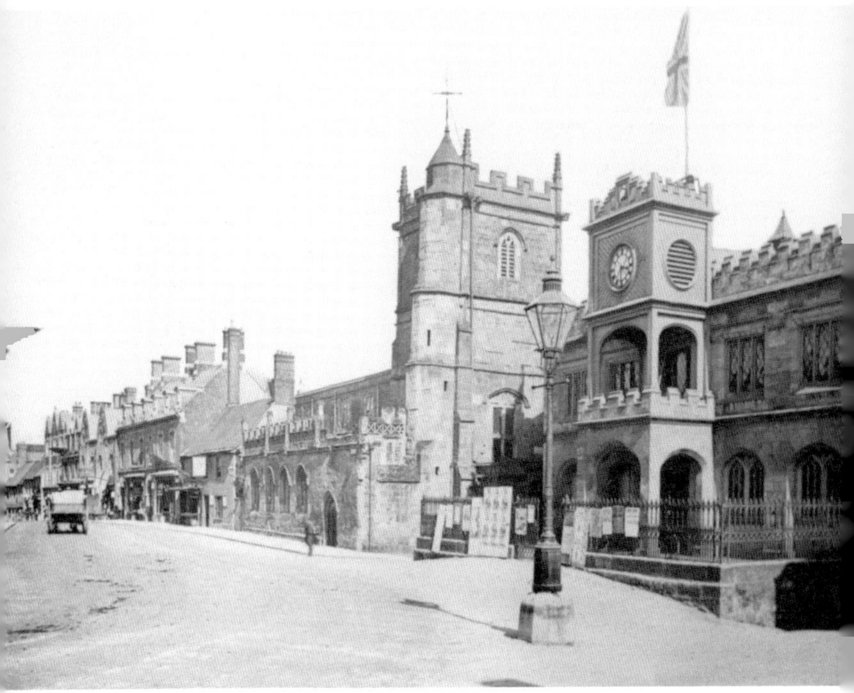

The hilltop town of Shaftesbury has wide views over the Blackmore Vale and thousands of acres of rolling Dorset countryside. Some locals still use its old name of Shaston. Alfred the Great and Edmund Ironside endowed Shaftesbury's abbey with buildings and land, and Alfred's daughter was the abbess. Edward the Martyr was buried at the abbey and King Canute died whilst staying there.

SHAFTESBURY

THE TOWN HALL AND ST PETER'S CHURCH c1902 / S593501

Sherborne is, by some people's estimation, the most beautiful of the Dorset towns. It is certainly a settlement of considerable historic interest: it has connections with a number of characters from English history, including Saxon kings, Cardinal Wolsey, Sir Walter Raleigh and Oliver Cromwell.

SHERBORNE

FROM THE SLOPES 1895 / 37076

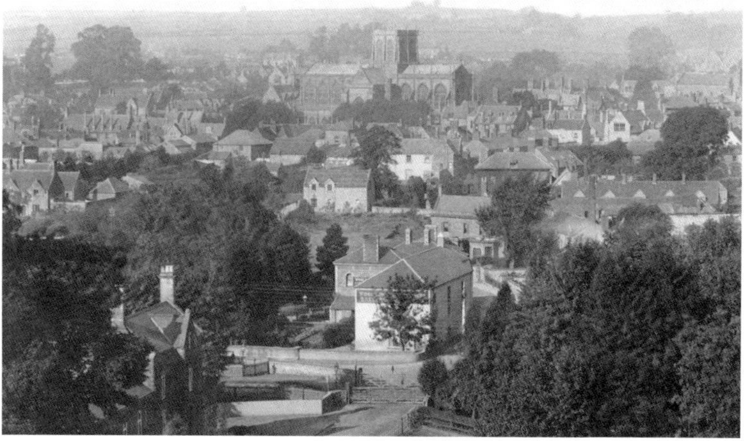

In Cheap Street is the Conduit, originally situated in the cloisters of Sherborne Abbey and used as a washing house, or lavatorium. The Conduit was moved to its present location after the dissolution of the religious house and used as a market building. It has since served as a police station, reading room and bank.

SHERBORNE

CHEAP STREET 1903 / 49719

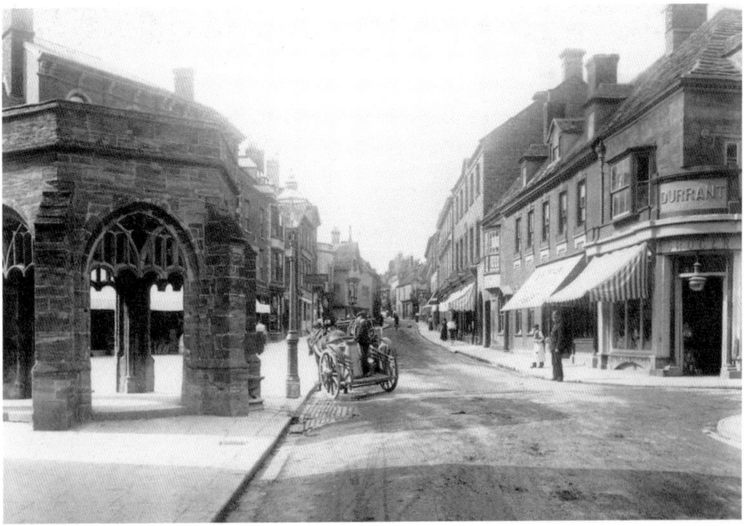

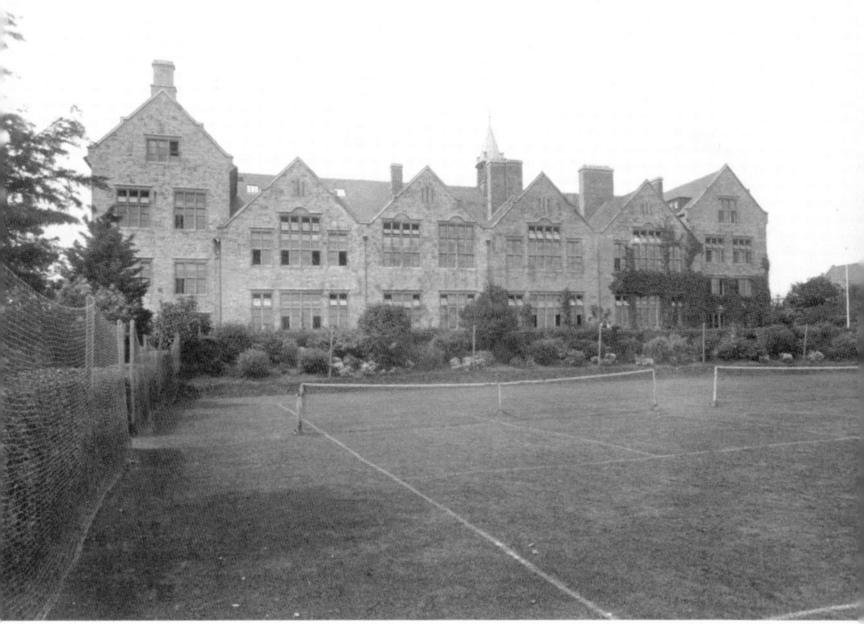

Sherborne is famous for its public schools, and on most days in term time pupils can be seen threading their way around the old town. The presence of the schools gives Sherborne an academic air, rather like an old university town.

SHERBORNE

SHERBORNE SCHOOL FOR GIRLS 1912 / 64658

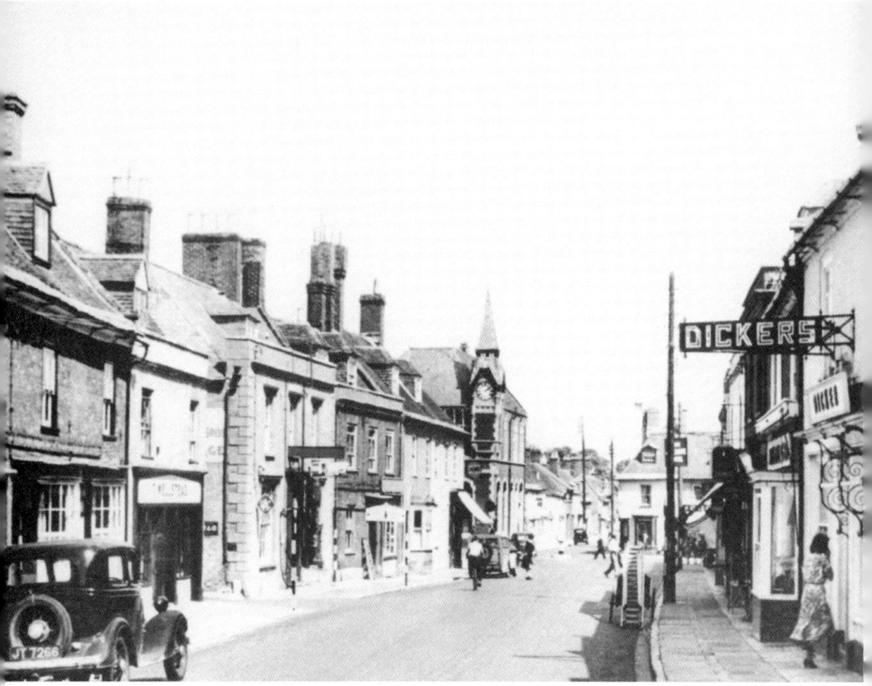

The Romans originally laid out the streets of Wareham to match the four points of the compass. The street names of today, North, South, East and West, match this design. Most of the buildings seen here date from after the great fire which destroyed Wareham in 1762.

WAREHAM

WEST STREET 1949 / W173035

Thomas Hardy lived in Wimborne for a short period during his first marriage. The town features slightly in his novel 'Two on a Tower', which was written at that time. Hardy was fond of sitting in the Minster with only the organist and his music for company.

WIMBORNE

HIGH STREET 1904 / 52472

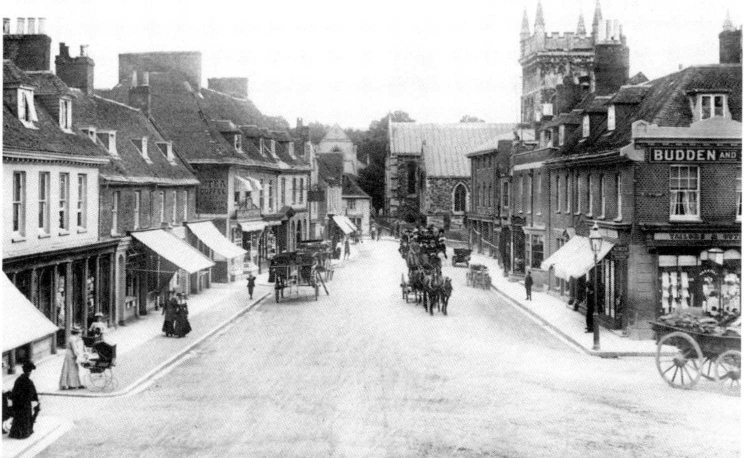

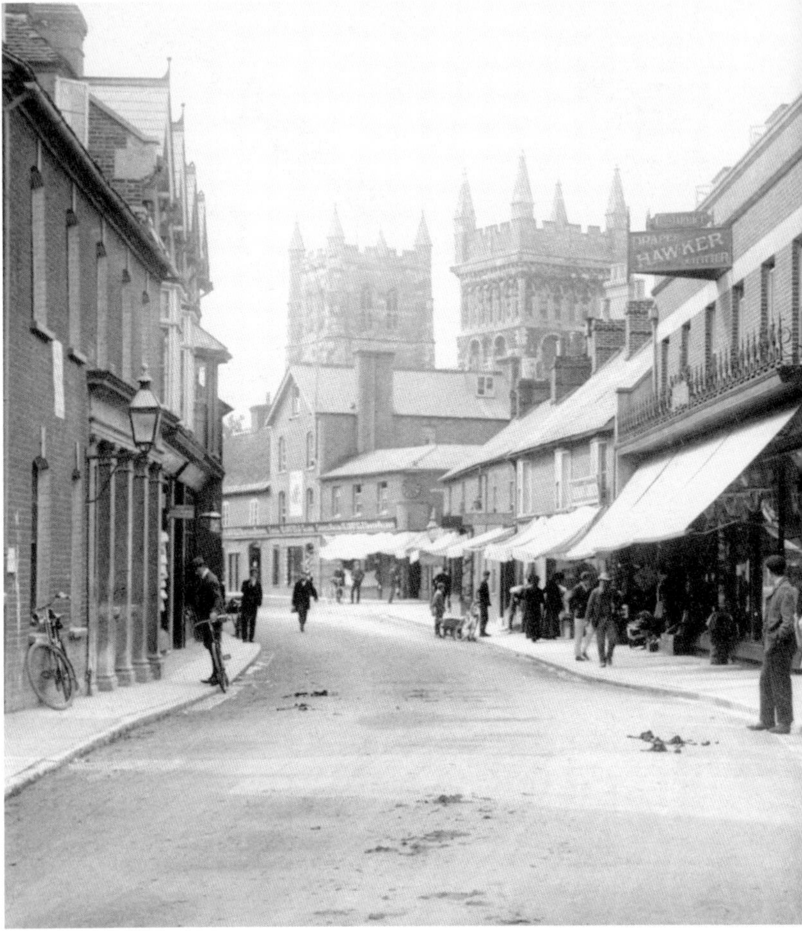

WIMBORNE

EAST STREET 1904 / 52475

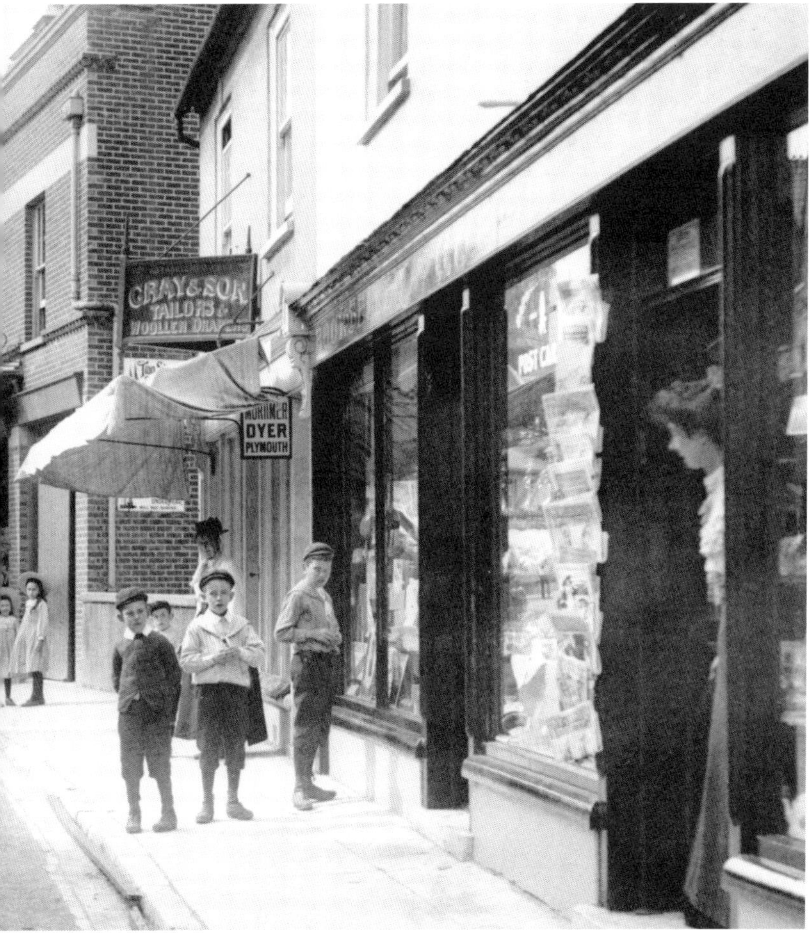

The visitor to Wimborne today will find it hard to imagine the streets being as empty as this, with pedestrians and cyclists dominating the scene. This is Wimborne as Thomas Hardy, a keen cyclist, would have known it thirty years earlier.

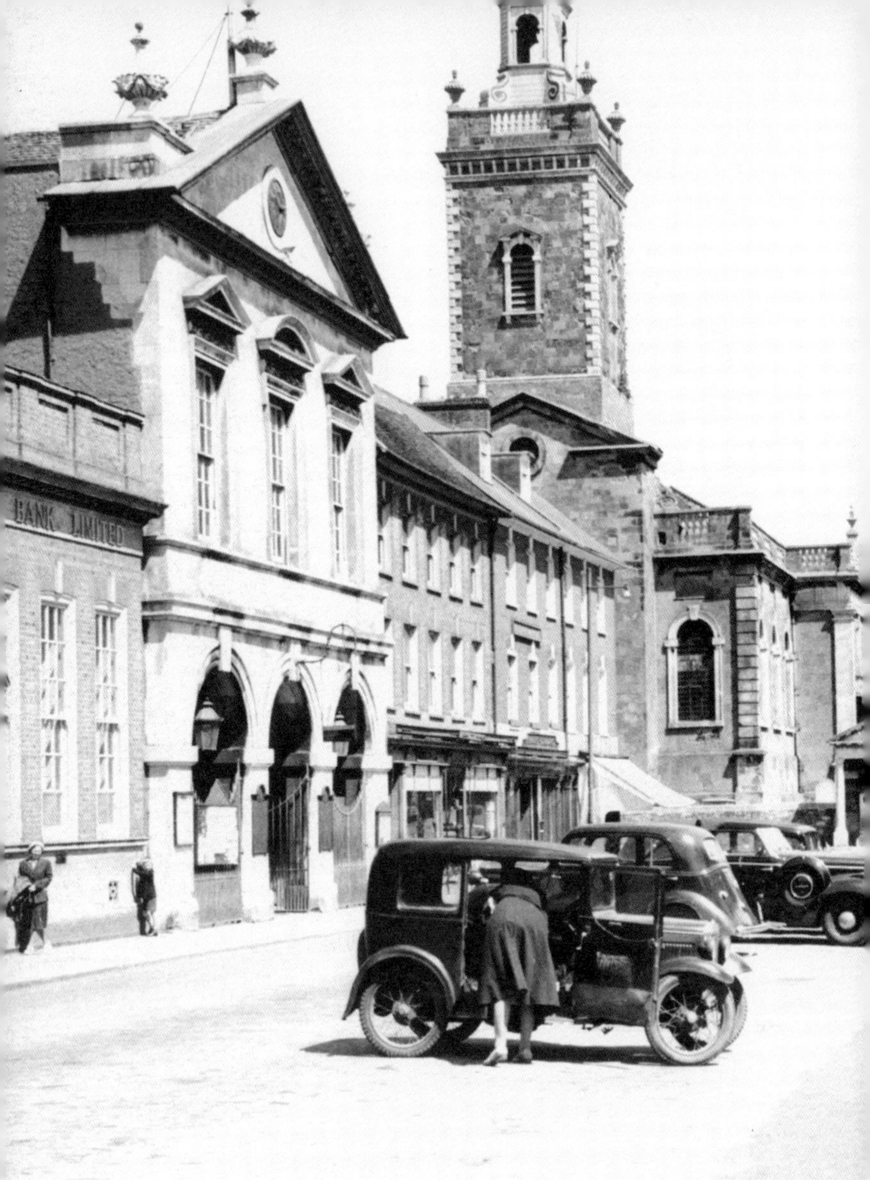
BANK LIMITED

BLANDFORD FORUM

MARKET PLACE 1950 / B282003

The market place at Blandford held important sheep fairs until well into the 20th century, with the town council taking a toll on all sales. Blandford has declined as an agricultural centre, but is a popular shopping venue for the inhabitants of the surrounding villages.

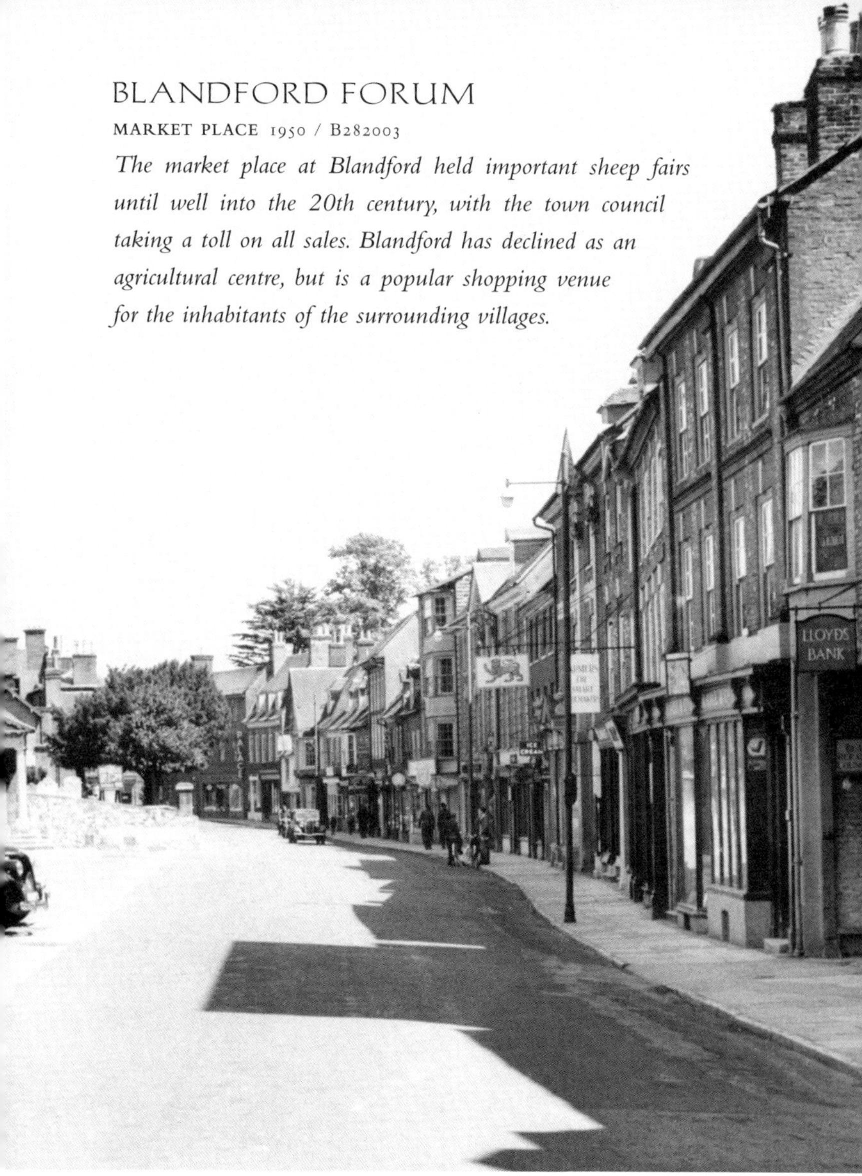

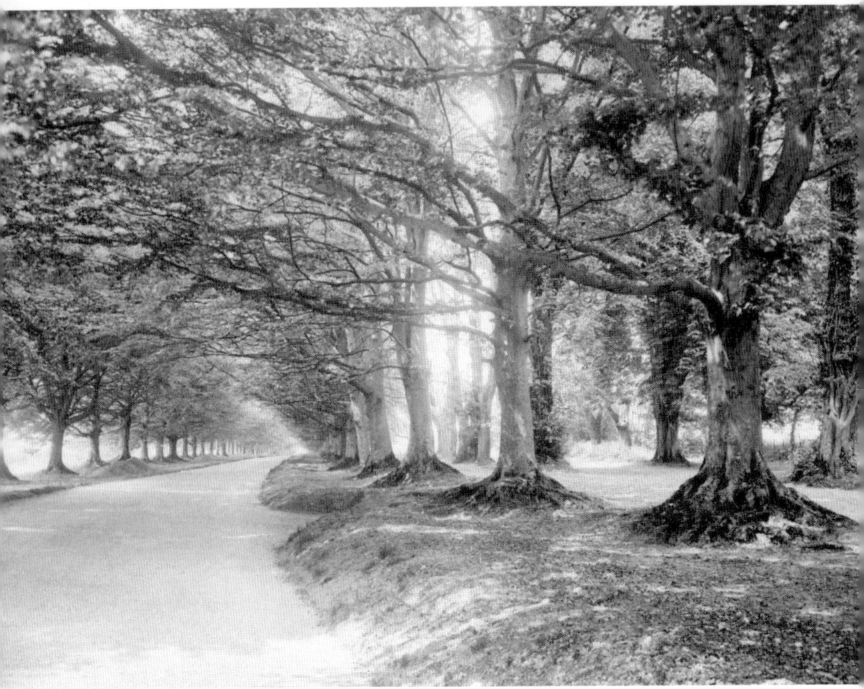

The long avenue of beech trees which lines the road beyond Wimborne, towards the ancient hillfort of Badbury Rings, is one of the finest sights in England. In the autumn, the overhanging branches form a seemingly never-ending tunnel of gold as the traveller journeys onward.

BADBURY RINGS

THE AVENUE OF TREES 1936 / 87209

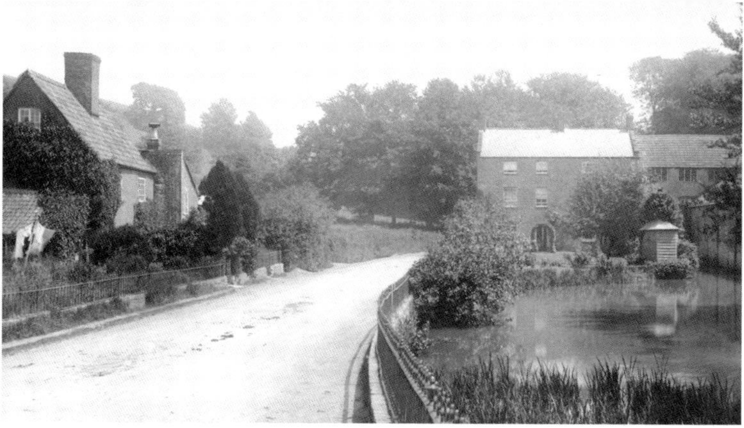

ALLINGTON, THE VILLAGE 1902 / 48399

THE RURAL HEARTLAND

DORSET'S RURAL HEARTLAND is best explored on foot, for walking the lanes and paths which thread from village to village is the only way to seek out the scenes captured at a vital time in their history by the Frith photographer. Other forms of transport are too swift: the greater delights of Dorset's scenery are missed by using them. Each mile of the way, you will know that you are treading in the footsteps of Iron Age man, Roman legions, quarrymen, farmers and poets. It says a lot for this landscape that artists of all kinds have responded to it and interpreted it in diverse ways.

This rural hinterland is both beautiful and mysterious, filled with history and crammed with legend. Until the 19th century it would seldom have been visited by the outsider; its deep wooded valleys, chalk downlands and secluded heaths form a physical and mental barrier to the intruder. The locals themselves would hardly have strayed much beyond their villages, except to visit nearby market towns, or to drive livestock from parish to parish along the ancient droving routes which can still be followed today. Only the adventurous minority—tinkers, smugglers, rebels and the gentry—would have gone further.

Life in these agricultural communities was not always a pastoral idyll. Many of the charming cottages we admire today, and which the Frith photographer captured so well, would have been rural slums a century or more ago, for the lot of the Dorset farmworker could be hard. Once, this peaceful landscape teemed with social agitation as the Swing Riots and the transportation of the Tolpuddle Martyrs brought dissent and rebellion to the village squares and green meadows of inland Dorset.

These communities must have witnessed similar upheavals throughout the centuries, lost as they are in time. Fortifications, from Iron Age hillfort to gaunt Norman castle, bear witness to earlier conflicts. But there was light as well as darkness. The churches, whose peals of bells sound sweetly over the surrounding downlands, show the peaceful energies of Saxon and Norman builders—and often the worst excesses of Victorian 'restorers'. The residents of a hundred manor houses shaped the landscape with their ordered parklands and pheasant preserves, sometimes removing whole villages to improve a view. Every plough and woodsman's axe has marked the land in some way, for the history of all society is writ large across this countryside.

Thomas Hardy captured all of this landscape in his series of Wessex novels, at a time before their character was changed by the intrusions of modern life and the deadening influence of far-distant urban philosophies. Only a child of the Dorset heathlands, as Hardy was, could have portrayed this lovely pastoral landscape with such accuracy and affection.

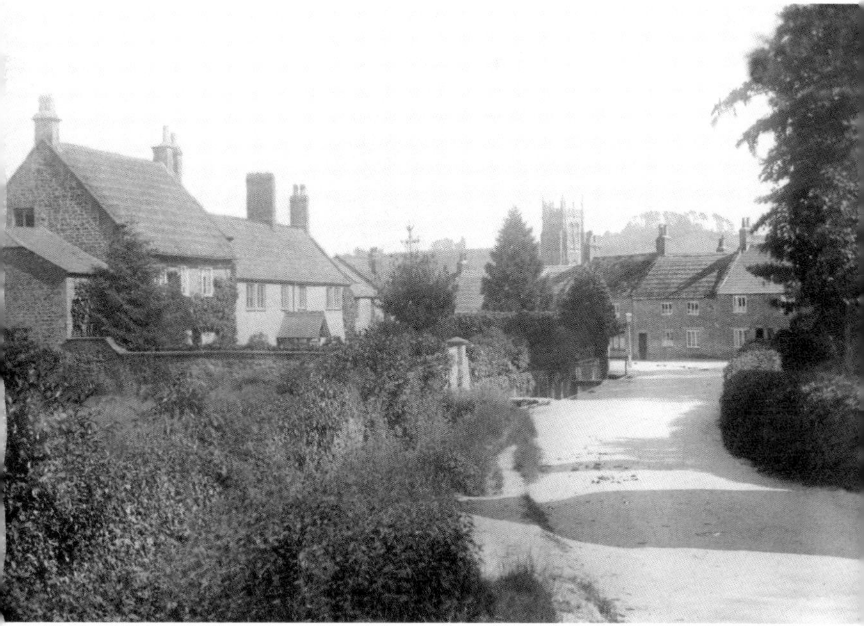

Beaminster today is not so very different from the old Dorset village that the dialect poet William Barnes would have known. Its name is always pronounced Be'mister as in Barnes's famous poem, and it remains the quaint old market town it always was.

BEAMINSTER

THE VILLAGE 1902 / 48422

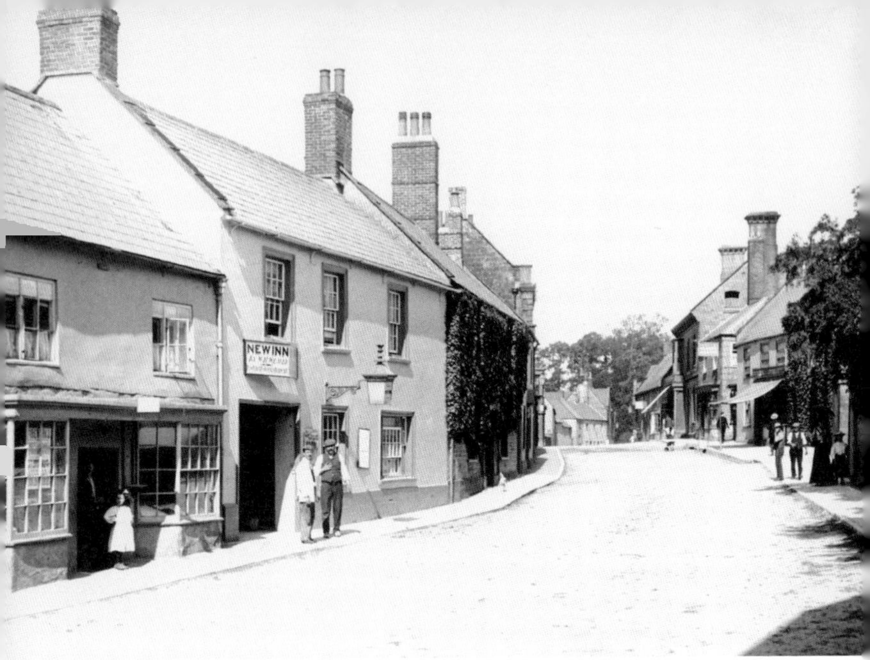

In its heyday, Beaminster could boast at least seventeen inns, built to cater for the many farmers who came to town for the weekly market, as well as passengers on the Crewkerne to Bridport coach. The New Inn, shown here, was favoured by rural workers who would come to sample Mr Weaver's famous ales.

BEAMINSTER

HOGSHILL STREET 1902 / 48425

Beaminster is the 'Emminster' of Hardy's novel 'Tess of the D'Urbervilles'. Here was the home of Tess's estranged husband Angel Clare, and here Tess ended her long and fruitless walk across Dorset to meet the Clare family. Hardy drew a very accurate picture of Beaminster, and it is possible to follow in his heroine's footsteps.

BEAMINSTER

MARKET PLACE 1907 / 58134

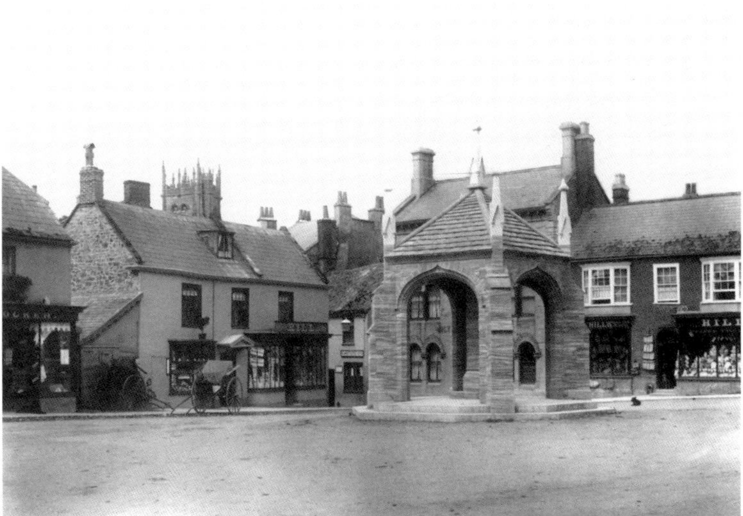

Bindon Abbey was the location of an important Cistercian monastery and dates back to 1172. Little remains of the original building; this neo-gothic gatehouse dates back only to the 1790s. It is the only part of the Abbey visible to the public.

BINDON ABBEY

THE GATEWAY 1894 / 34614

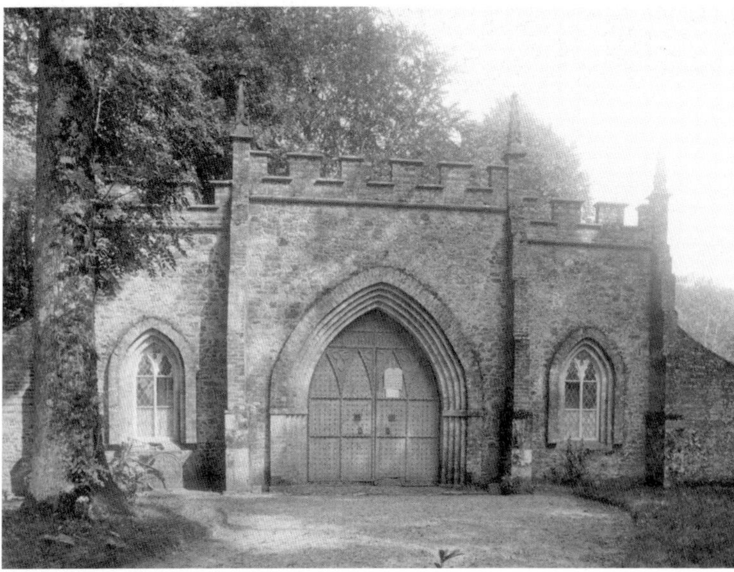

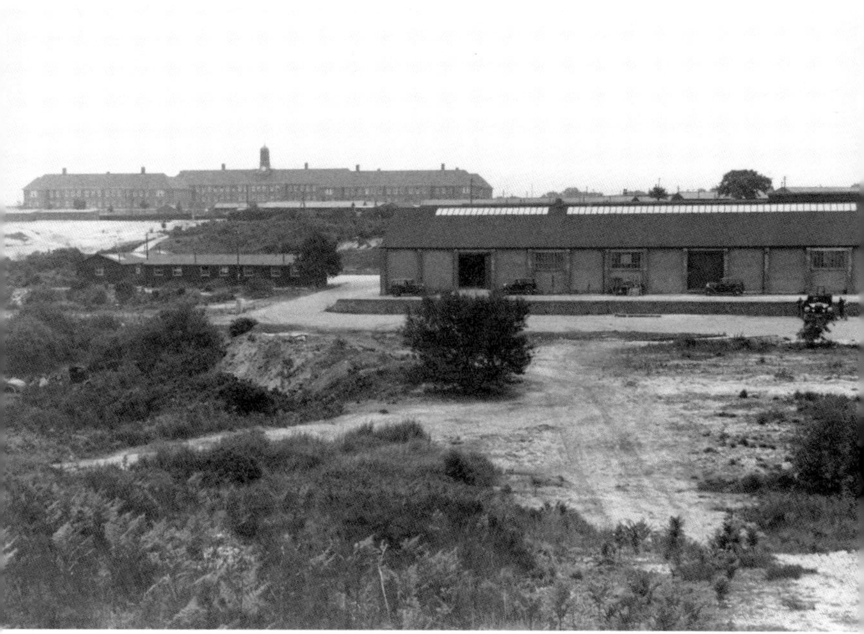

Bovington Camp dates back to the First World War, and is the home of the Royal Armoured Corps. The surrounding heathland is heavily used for tank training. It was in a hospital here that Lawrence of Arabia died following his motorcycle crash in 1935.

BOVINGTON

THE VIEW FROM THE TANK TRAINING GROUNDS C1955 / B734004

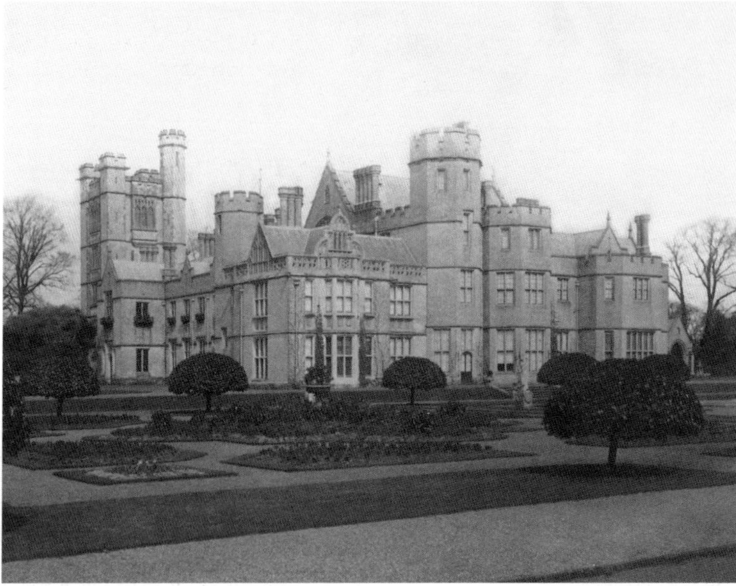

Canford Manor, not far from Wimborne, dates from the early years of the 19th century, though it stands on the site of an ancient house which once belonged to the Earls of Salisbury. The present building, now a public school, was for many years the country seat of Lord Wimborne.

CANFORD

THE MANOR c1886 / 19490

CHARMINSTER

THE CHURCH 1922 / 72760

The 15th-century tower of Charminster's church dominates the valley of the River Cerne, and was built under the direction of Sir Thomas Trenchard. Parts of the building date back to the 12th century. The wooden pulpit is three hundred and fifty years old.

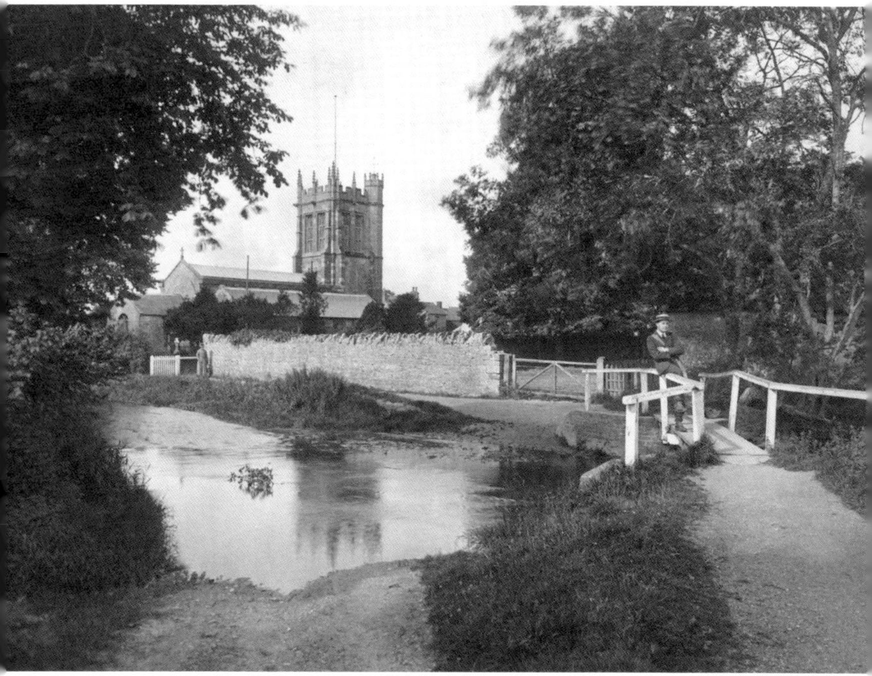

The ruins of Corfe Castle dominate the parish and village to which it has given its name. The original Saxon fortification was succeeded by the extensive Norman castle seen today. The castle held out for the king during the English Civil War, and attempts were made to 'slight' the castle afterwards. Although it was damaged, the castle resisted the massive destruction that was intended for it.

CORFE CASTLE

THE CASTLE AND THE VILLAGE 1890 / 25562

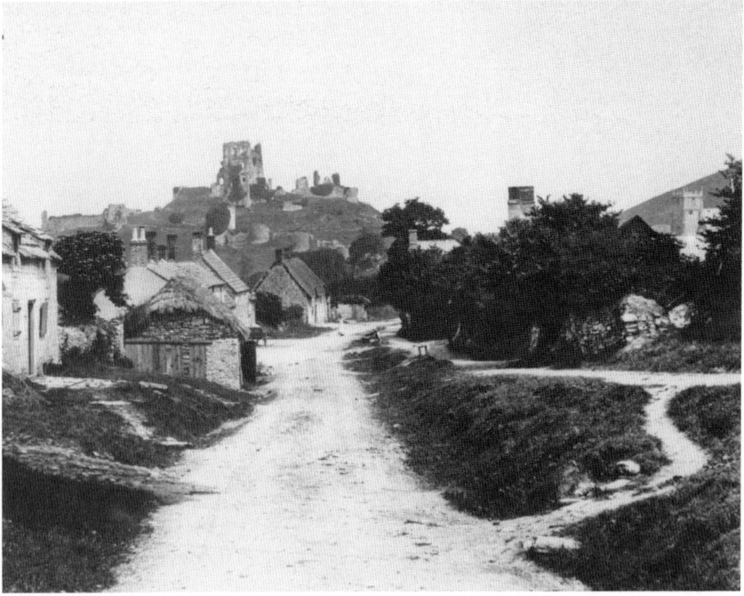

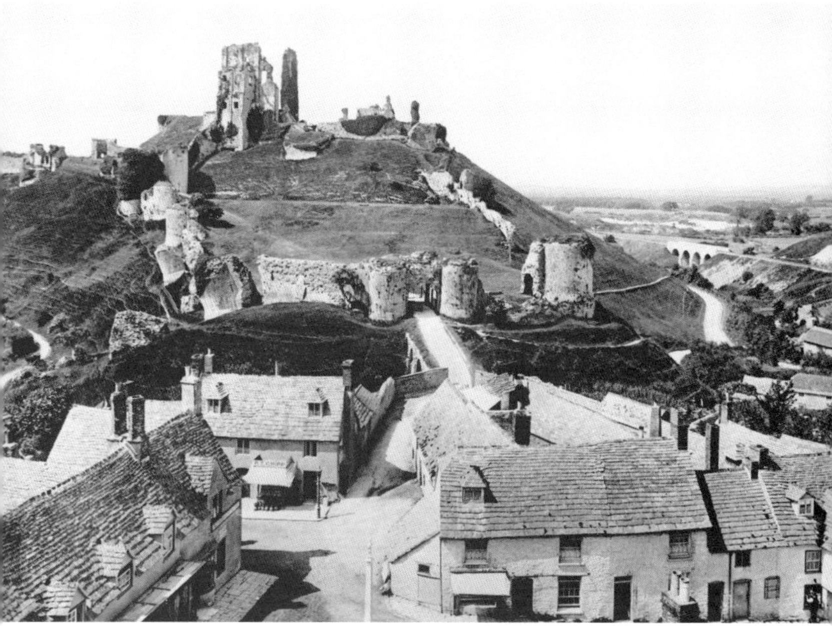

One of the darkest deeds in English history took place in Saxon times, when King Edward was murdered, probably by order of his stepmother, in 978. When hunting in this area, Edward called at the castle. Tradition says that his stepmother brought him a cup of wine and, as he drank, one of her servants stabbed the king in the back. The slain monarch was canonised as Edward the Martyr, and Corfe Church was dedicated to his memory.

CORFE CASTLE

FROM THE CHURCH 1897 / 40318

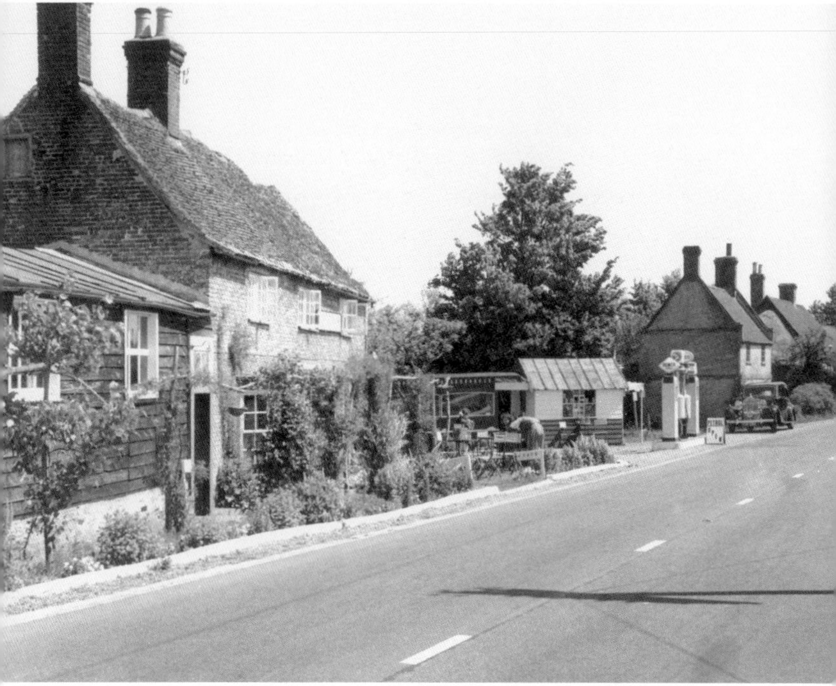

Corfe Mullen had a mill as long ago as the Domesday Book; it retained its independence until well into the 20th century, when its great neighbour Poole began to creep out towards it. Its greatest attraction, not shown here, is the delightful little 13th-century church.

CORFE MULLEN

OLD MILL TEA ROOMS c1955 / C596005

Thomas Hardy writes of a journey into Cranborne in 'Tess of the D'Urbervilles', where the present Fleur-de-Lys tavern is depicted as the much less salubrious 'Flower-de-Luce'. In the woodlands of the Chase, Tess is seduced by Alec D'Urberville, though Hardy's imagination makes the area much wilder than it would probably have been even in his day.

CRANBORNE

WIMBORNE STREET 1954 / C694013

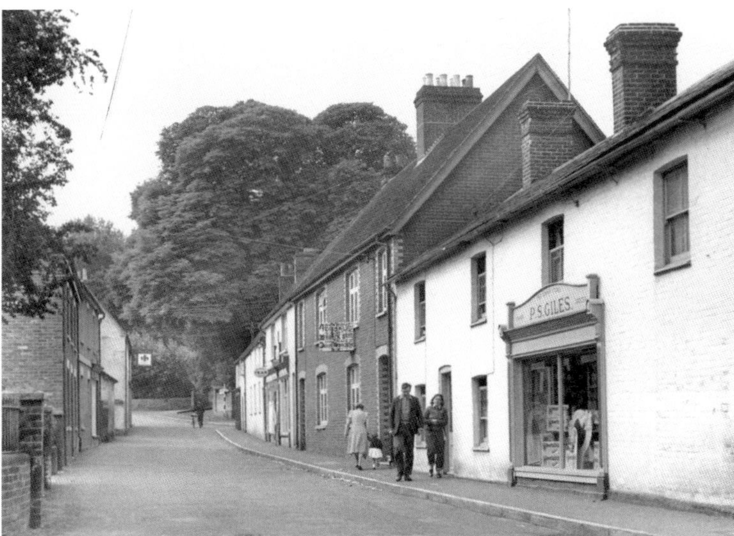

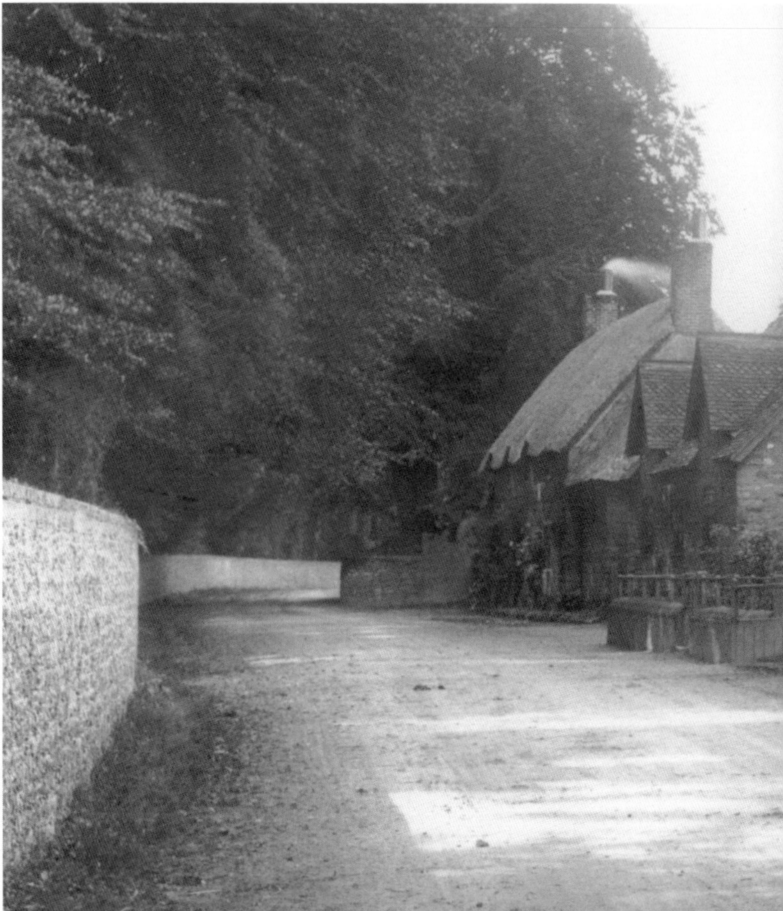

FRAMPTON

THE VILLAGE 1906 / 54584

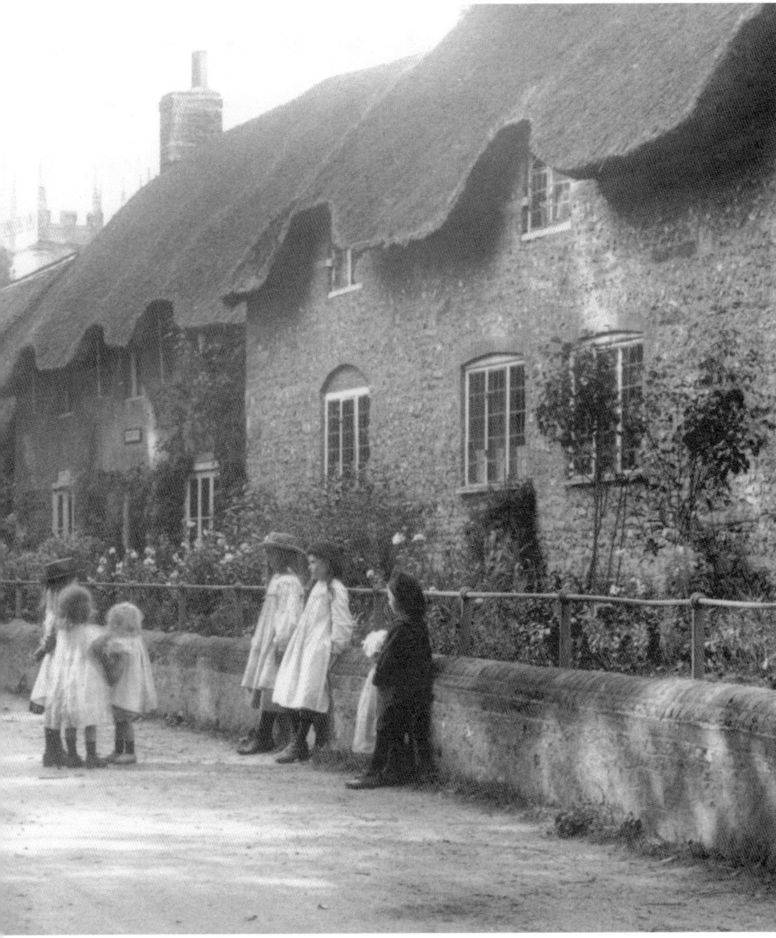

The rural poet William Barnes achieved national fame through the endeavours of Mrs Caroline Norton, who stayed here while the Dorset bard was living nearby at Winterbourne Came. Without her efforts, Barnes might never have been known beyond the bounds of his county.

Frampton, 'the settlement on the Frome', is an attractive downland village north-west of Dorchester. The old manor house of Frampton Court was demolished in 1939. In 1840 its then owner dismantled a large portion of the village to improve his view. There is a delicious irony in the fact that the village has now survived his house.

FRAMPTON

ST MARY'S CHURCH 1906 / 54585

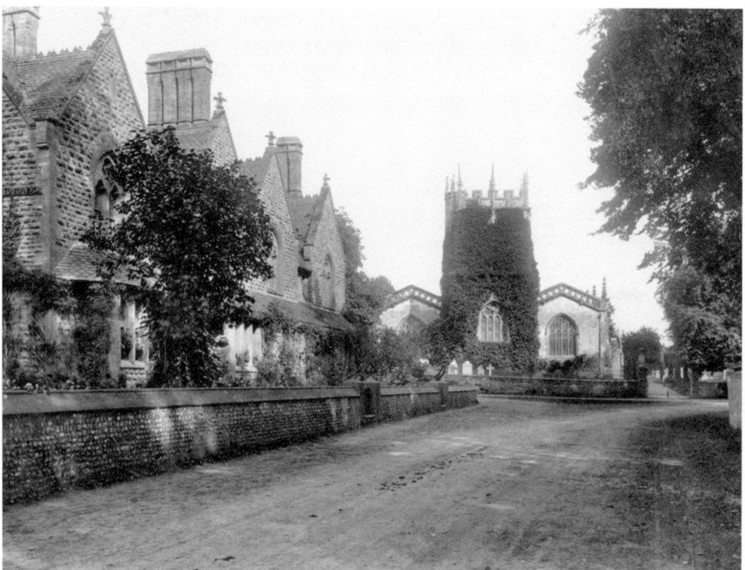

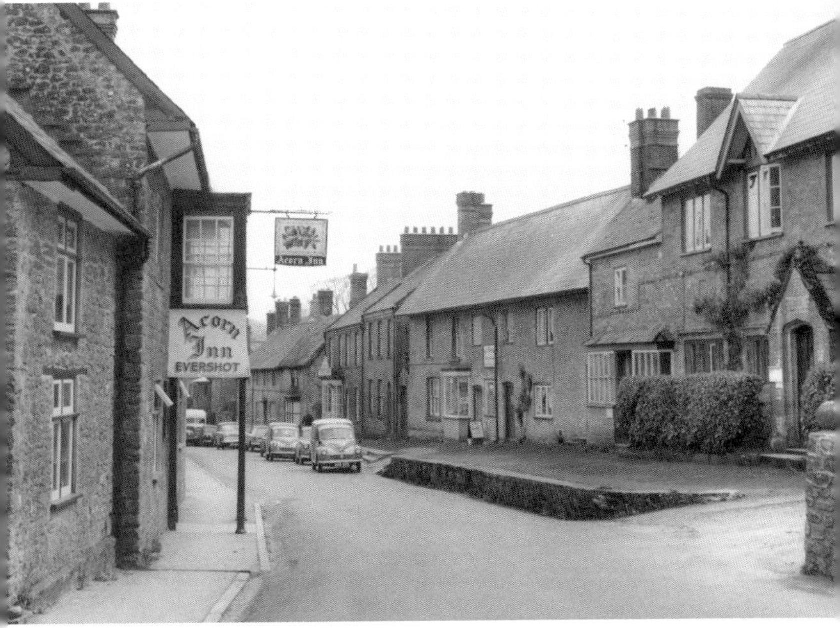

Situated on the high downlands where the flowing waters of St John's Spring become the source of the River Frome, Evershot had as its vicar in the 18th century the poet George Crabbe. The award of the living allowed Crabbe to marry, though he seldom visited the parish, sending a curate in his stead.

EVERSHOT

FORE STREET c1965 / E128015

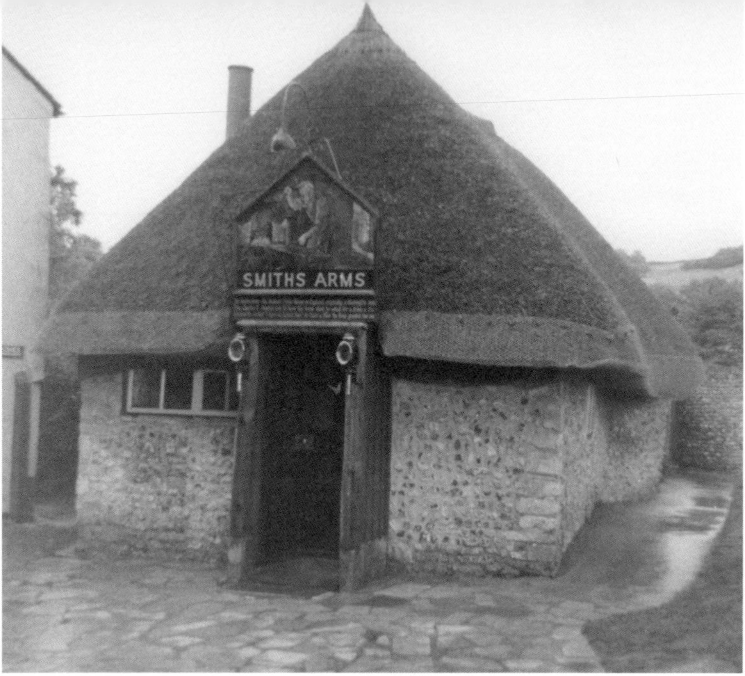

Once the village smithy, the inn at Godmanstone is said to be the smallest public house in England. The beautifully-thatched building measures only 20ft by 10ft; it is about 500 years old.

GODMANSTONE

THE SMITH'S ARMS C1955 / G179003

FROME VAUCHURCH

THE VILLAGE 1906 / 54575

This attractive waterside village was the home of the novelist and poet Sylvia Townsend Warner for over forty years. Its tiny towerless church stands sentinel over the cottages, gardens and meadows as it has done for some eight hundred years.

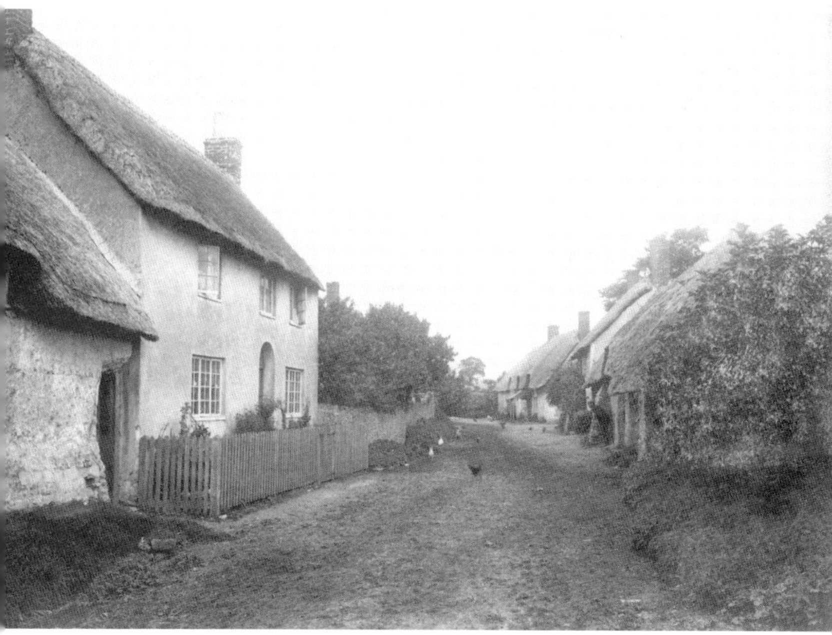

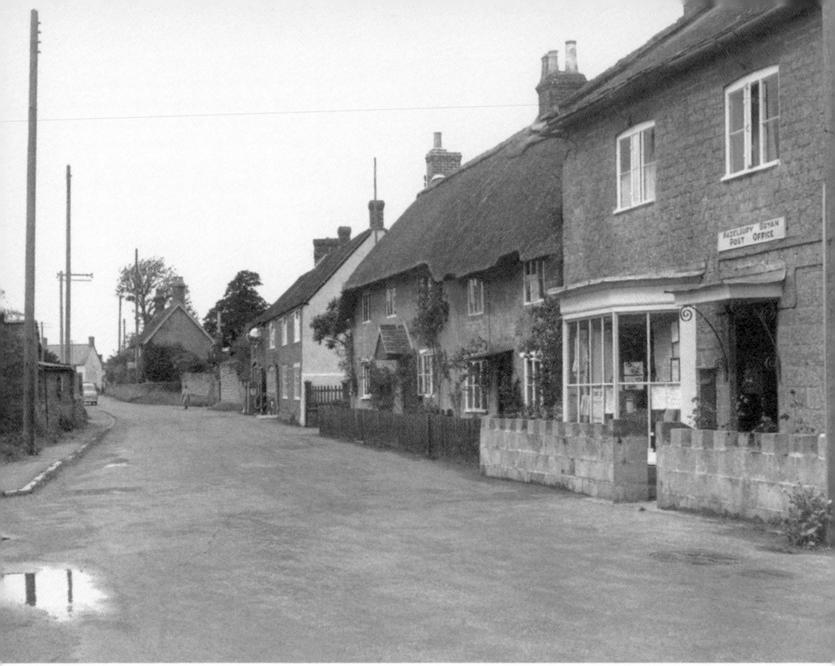

This village sprawls around the lanes of the surrounding countryside of the Blackmoor Vale as though not quite sure where it wants to be. The hilltop church dates back to at least the 14th century, and some of the cottages are of similar antiquity.

HAZELBURY BRYAN

THE POST OFFICE C1955 / H294007

Two miles south of Bulbarrow, one of Dorset's highest summits, Hilton and neighbouring Milton Abbas share some of the most beautiful countryside in the county. The thatched cottages, fascinating church and wonderful landscapes make Hilton a delightful place to linger.

HILTON

THE VILLAGE C1955 / H158004

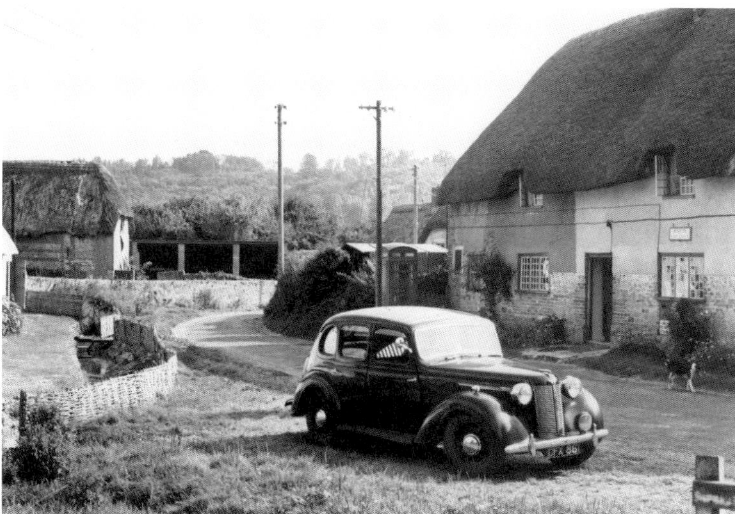

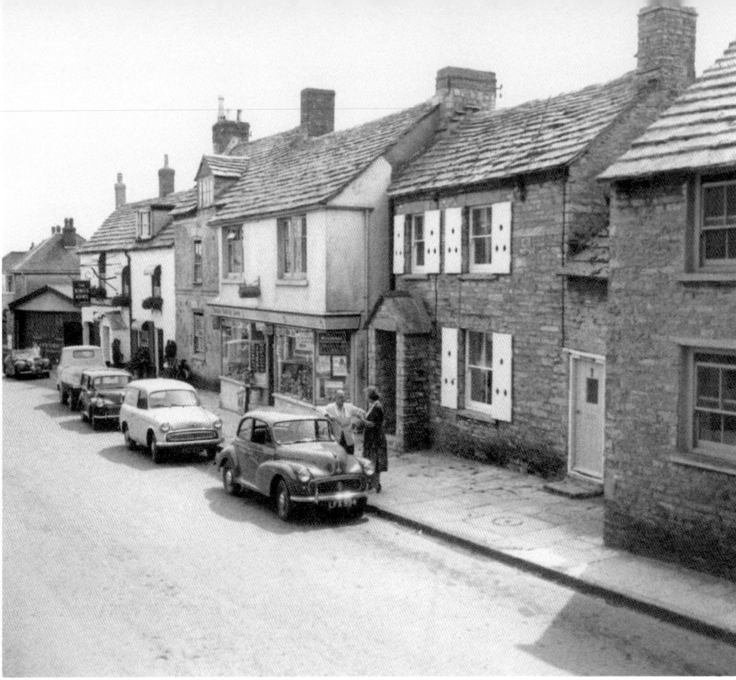

Once largely occupied by stoneworkers from the nearby stone quarries, this village stretches along the highway for a considerable distance, hence its name, a corruption of 'Longtown'. The Matravers family were considerable landowners on the Isle of Purbeck, and one Matravers was bloodily involved in the murder of Edward II.

LANGTON MATRAVERS

THE KING'S ARMS AND HIGH STREET c1965 / L469032

LITTON CHENEY

THE VILLAGE 1906 / 54543

Litton Cheney has a charming collection of Stuart and Georgian cottages strung out along its winding streets. Tiny brooks fill the air with the sound of running water. Its church is a fascinating medieval survival, which somehow escaped the worst excesses of Victorian restorers.

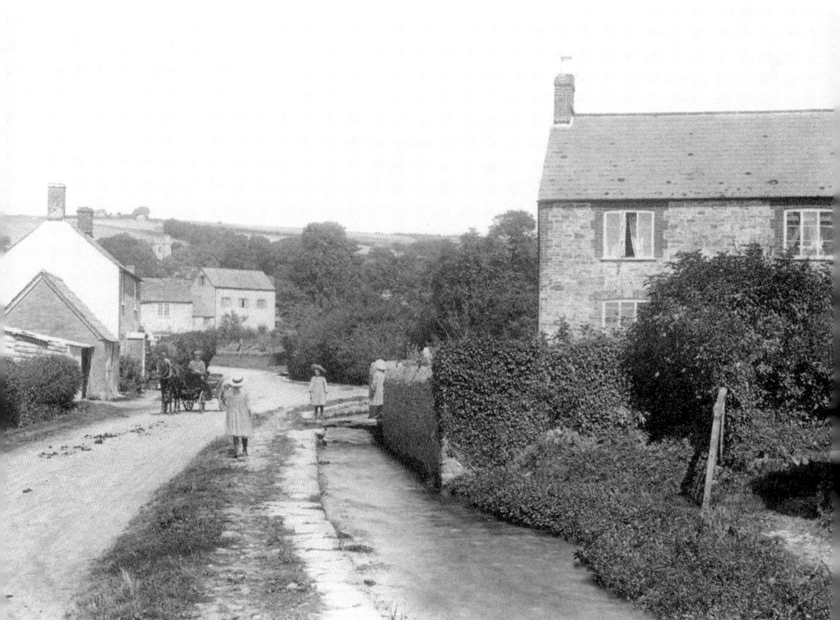

Loders was built in the domain of a Benedictine priory founded by the Norman grandee Baldwin de Redvers during the reign of Henry I. The present parish church formerly served the priory; the beautiful gardens of Loders Court surround the church.

LODERS

THE VILLAGE 1903 / 50496

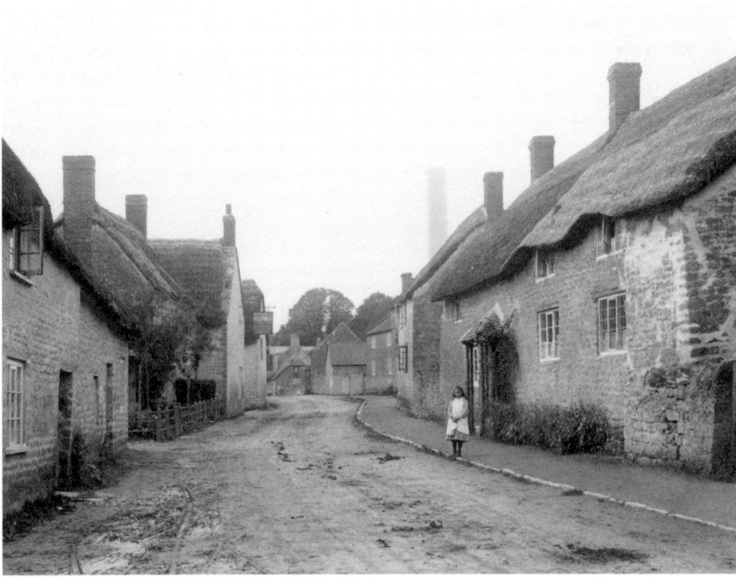

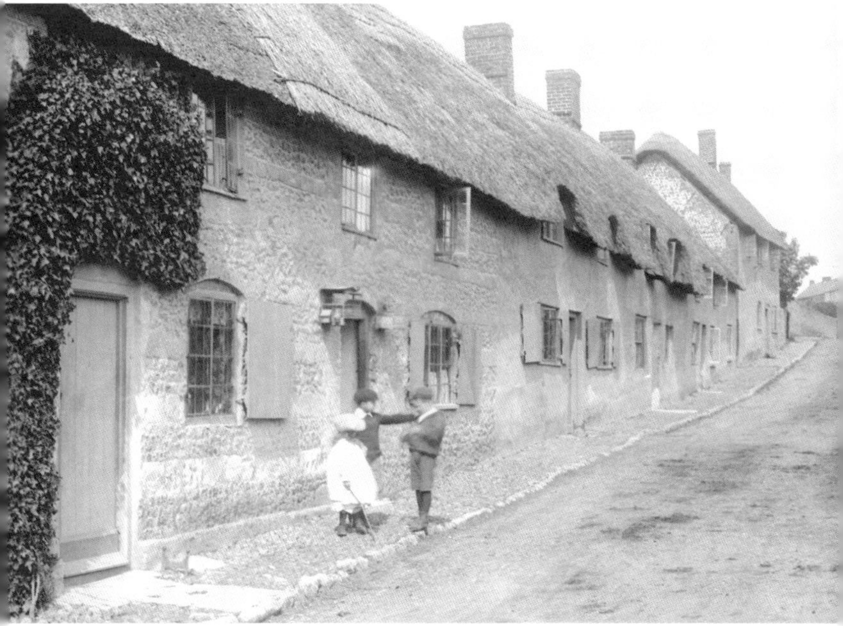

The working lives of the Dorset labourers who lived in cottages like these was hard, with poor wages and long hours. One of Thomas Hardy's few forays into politics was to champion the cause of better treatment for rural workers.

MAIDEN NEWTON

THE VILLAGE 1906 / 54567

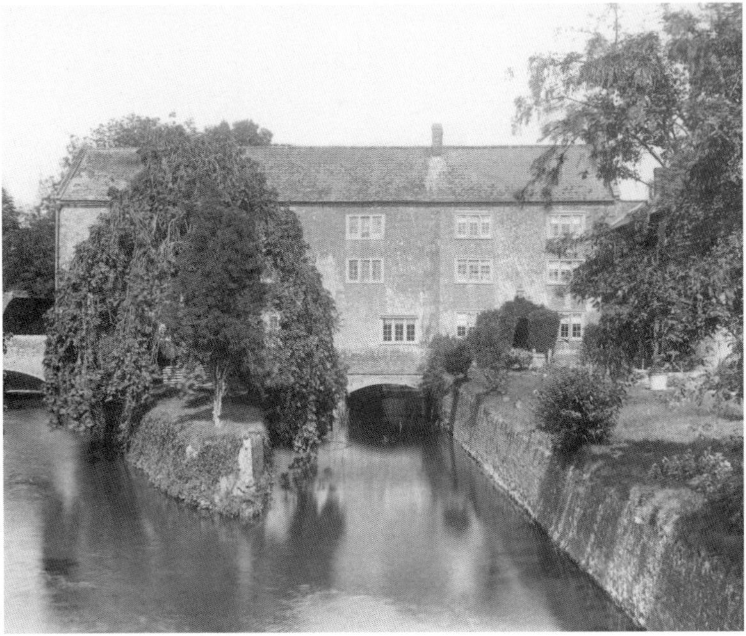

Maiden Newton's mill is probably situated on the site of many earlier mill buildings. There are records of settlements here dating back to the Roman occupation. This mill became a carpet factory in the 20th century.

MAIDEN NEWTON

THE MILL 1906 / 54570

MAIDEN NEWTON

DORCHESTER ROAD 1906 / 54563

Maiden Newton makes a good centre for exploring the Dorset downs. Many visitors walk up to the Iron Age hillfort of Eggardon. One such rambler was Thomas Hardy, who famously used the ramparts as a setting in his novel 'The Trumpet Major'.

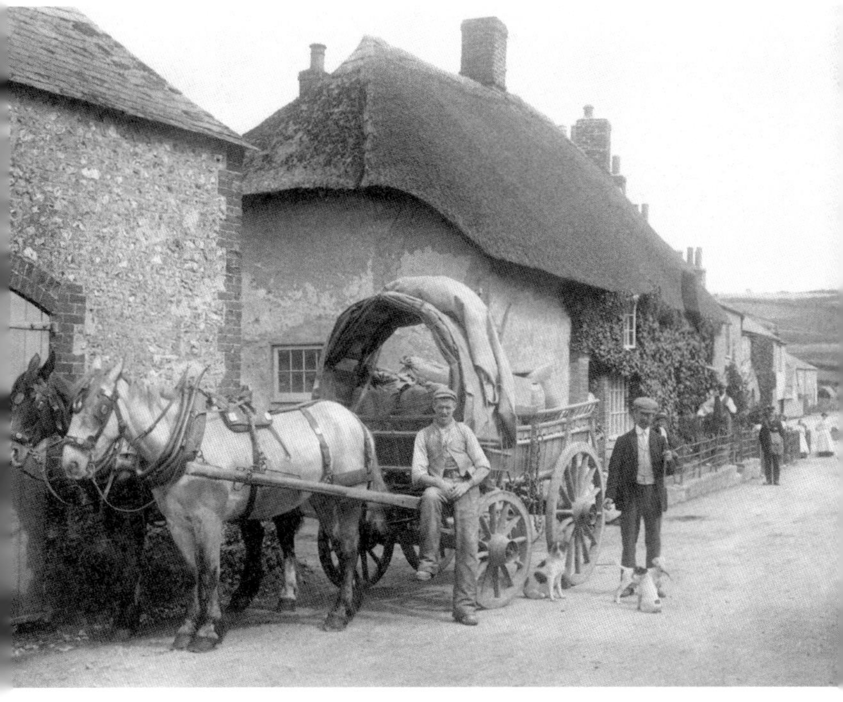

Melbury Osmond is mentioned in the Domesday Book as belonging to the Arundell family. It stayed in their possession until about a century ago. Thomas Hardy's parents were married in the village church in 1839.

MELBURY OSMOND

THE POST OFFICE c1955 / M216004

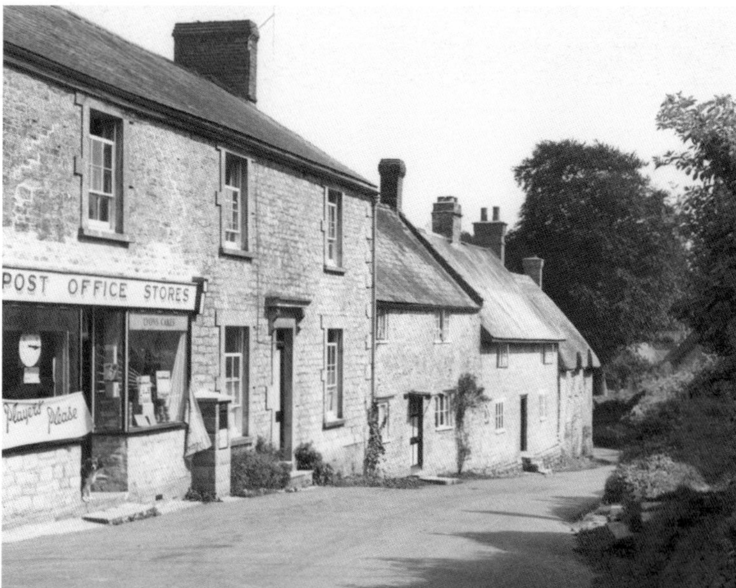

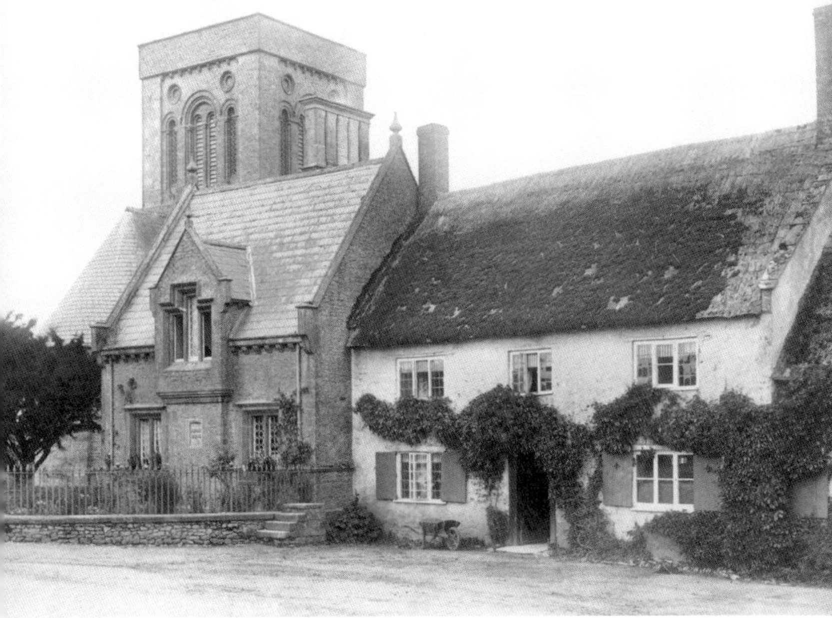

Melplash church may look vaguely Norman in design, but in fact it is less than two hundred years old. Unkind visitors have commented that the stout building resembles a water tower!

MELPLASH

THE CHURCH AND THE SCHOOL 1907 / 58148

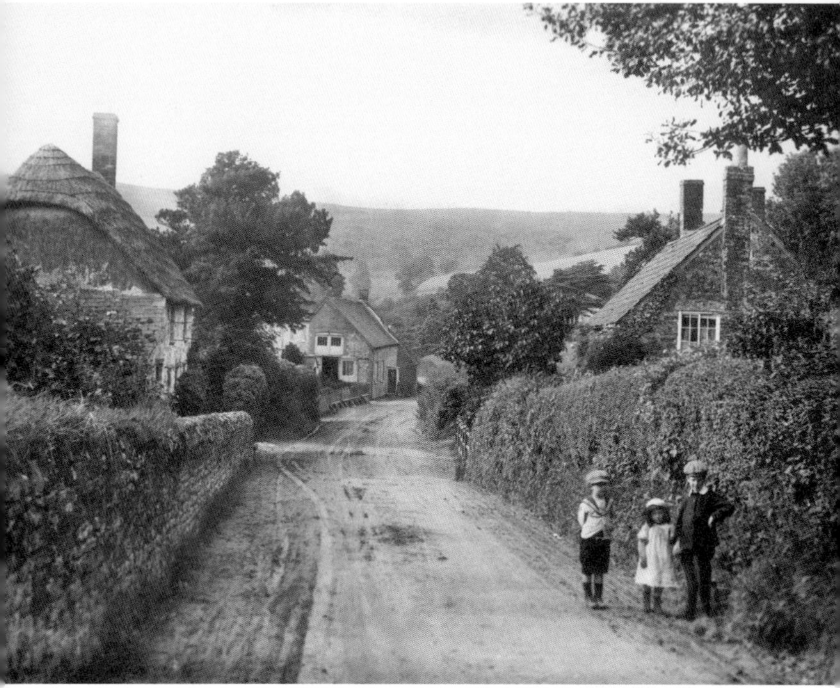

Melplash's only real claim on history is the story of Sir Thomas More (a distant relative of the saint): when he was Sheriff of Dorset, he freed all the prisoners from Dorchester gaol. More had to give both Melplash and his favourite daughter to Lord Paulet, who interceded with the king on his behalf in search of a pardon.

MELPLASH

THE VILLAGE 1912 / 65063

When the first Earl of Dorchester purchased Milton Abbey in 1752, he had the entire village dismantled, moving it further away from his new home. The picturesque village we see today with its carefully-tended gardens is the result of his quest for privacy.

MILTON ABBAS

THE VILLAGE c1955 / M80049

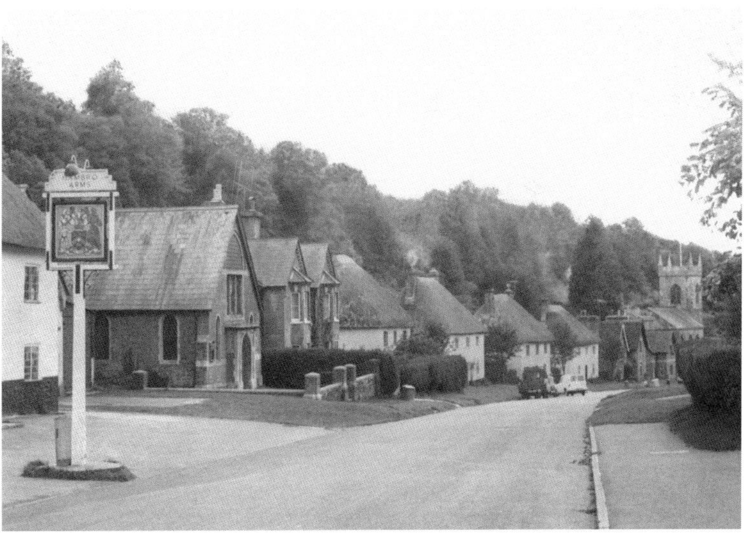

Morcombelake, situated on the high road between Lyme Regis and Bridport, is now famous as the home of the Moore's biscuit factory. The village itself is unjustly ignored by most travellers, who would do well to halt awhile to explore its buildings and the delightful countryside nearby.

MORCOMBELAKE

THE VILLAGE 1904 / 52774

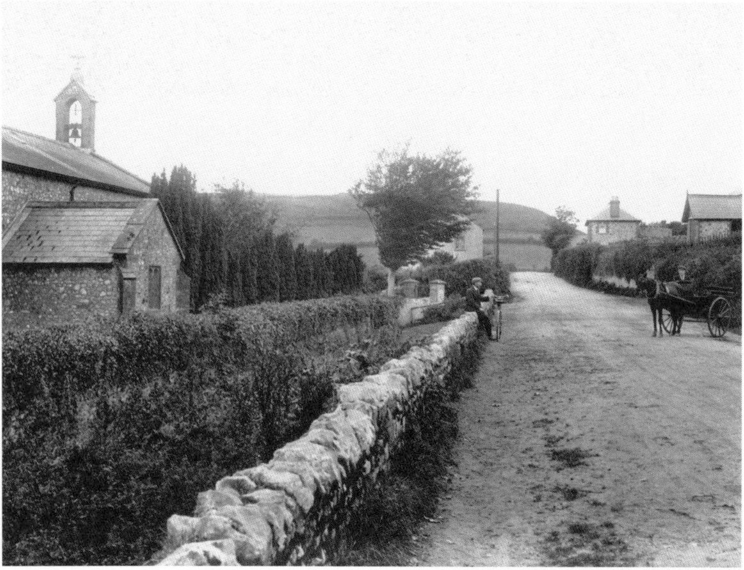

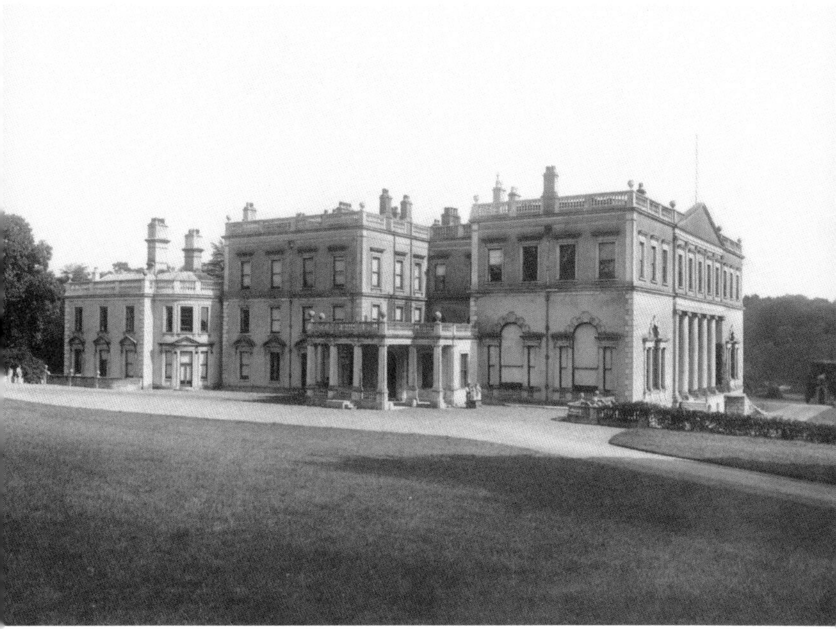

Princess Charlotte, the only child of the loveless marriage between George IV and Caroline of Brunswick, made Crichel House her home for a time. This popular princess died at the age of 21. Had she lived, she would have been Queen of England instead of Victoria, and the whole course of world history might have been different.

MORE CRICHEL

CRICHEL HOUSE 1904 / 52745

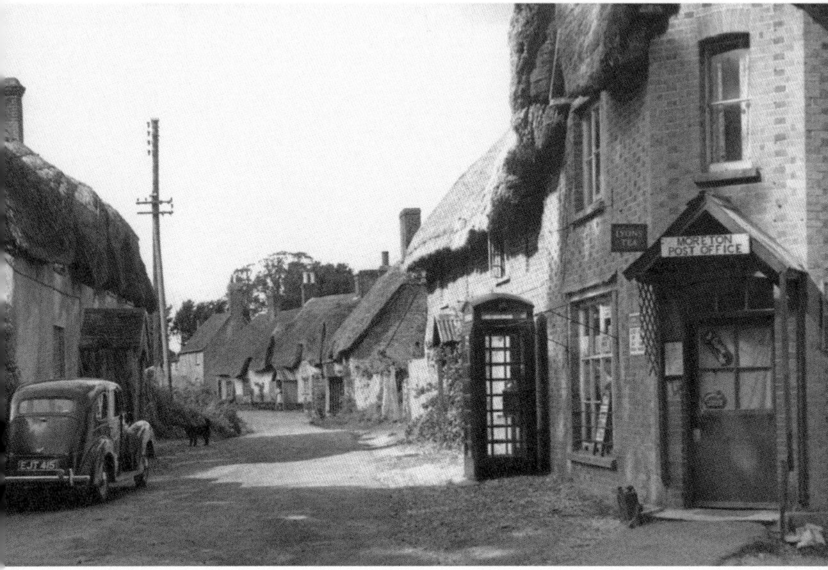

Moreton is the last resting place of Lawrence of Arabia, who lived nearby at Cloud's Hill. He died on the Bovington road in May 1935 riding his beloved motorcycle. Seventy years later, pilgrims still make the journey to pay homage at his grave.

MORETON

THE POST OFFICE c1955 / M308008

Athelhampton Hall is one of two grand houses near to the village of Puddletown, both lived in at various times by members of the Martyn family. The village church has many memorials to this longstanding local family.

PUDDLETOWN

ATHELHAMPTON HALL C1955 / P163046

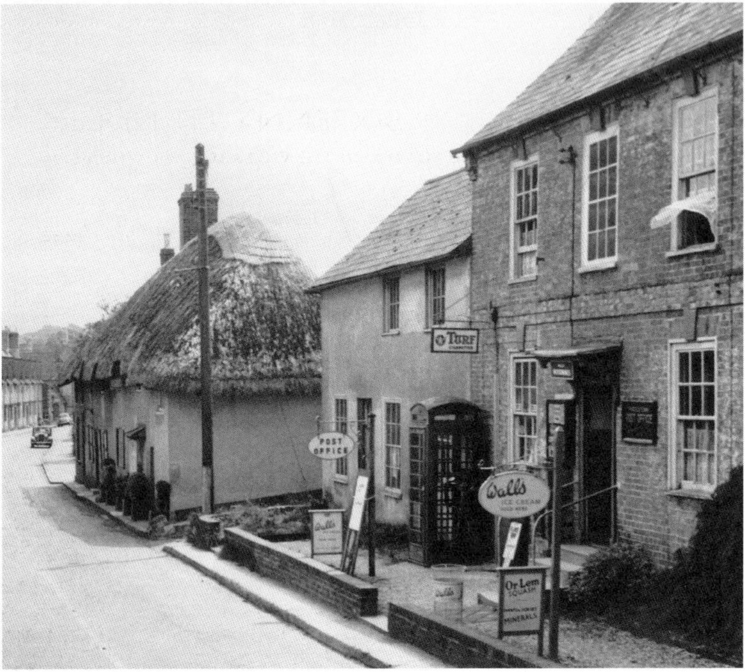

Puddletown is the 'Weatherbury' of Thomas Hardy's 'Far From the Madding Crowd'. This area is rich in Hardy associations. Much of Puddletown was rebuilt in 1864, but the area around the church suggests the village that the young Hardy would have known.

PUDDLETOWN

HIGH STREET c1955 / P163043

SIXPENNY HANDLEY

THE POND AND THE VICARAGE c1935 / S794006

This is a timeless photograph. This fine study of a horse and cart at Handley Pond portrays a rural scene that could have been observed at any period during the last several centuries. The man in the cart has recently been identified as carpenter and smallholder Alexander ('Billy') Day, who played the double bass in the village band.

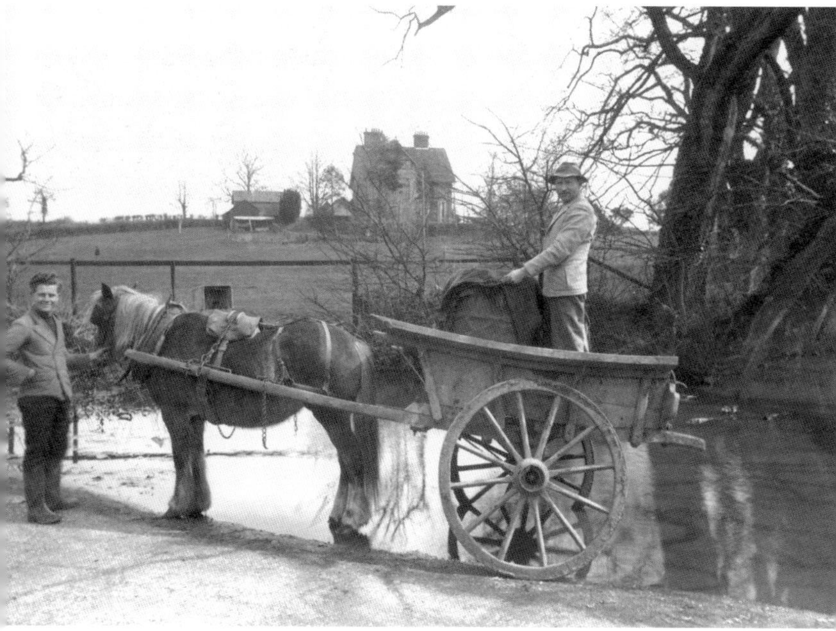

Though restored in 1855, the church at Tolpuddle is nine centuries old. In the north transept is a memorial carved in Purbeck stone to a 12th century priest called Phillip. In the churchyard is the last resting place of James Hammett, the only Tolpuddle Martyr to return to live in his home village. The others eventually emigrated to Canada after being pardoned.

TOLPUDDLE

THE CHURCH OF ST JOHN THE EVANGELIST C1955 / T154010

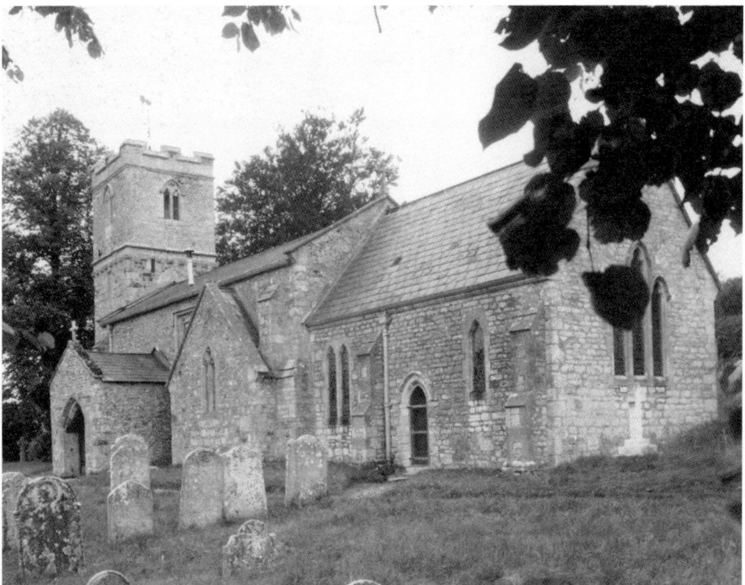

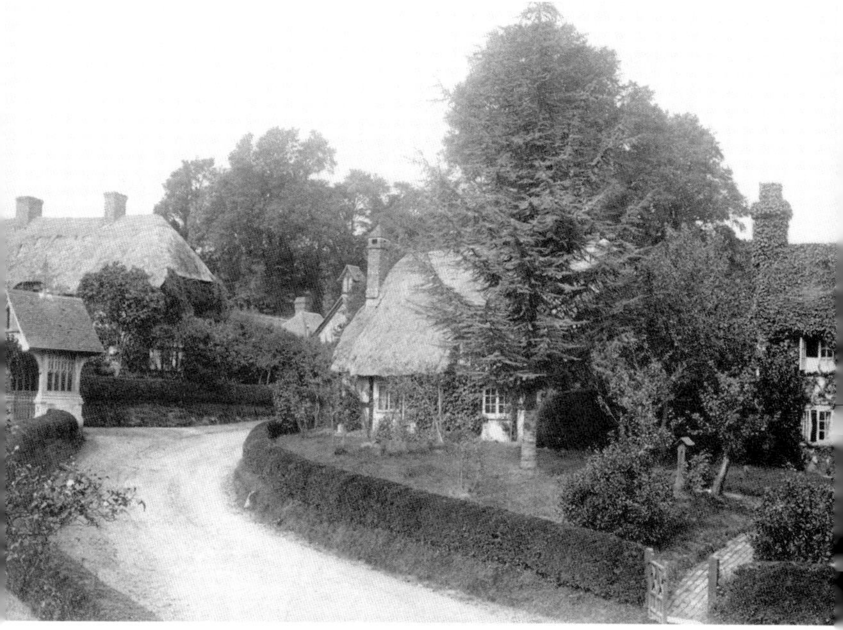

This fine brick-built village is one of north Dorset's loveliest, its cottage gardens a delight all year round. Even with modern day traffic it seems a place lost in time.

WITCHAMPTON

THE VILLAGE 1904 / 52739

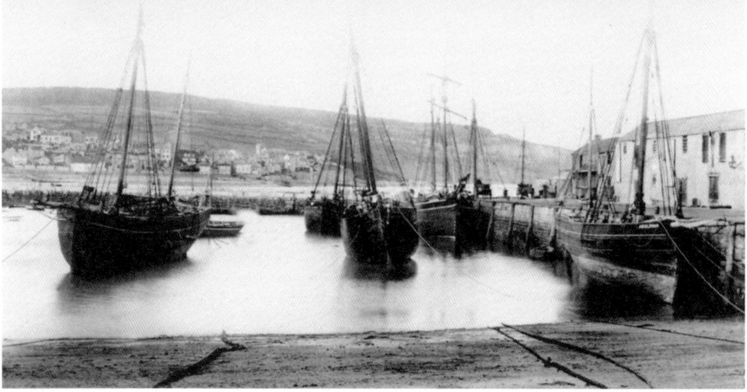

LYME REGIS, THE HARBOUR 1892 / 31308

ALONG THE COAST

AS YOU JOURNEY eastwards from the sedate and literary little town of Lyme Regis towards the sandy beaches and urban sprawl of Bournemouth, you become aware that this beautiful Dorset coast has been created by the happy amalgamation of the best of nature and the sympathetic handling of the original creation by humankind, for this is very much a worked landscape. Generations of farmers have grazed and tilled the ground, but much more gently than in many parts of England, using methods not so different from those used by their distant ancestors. The coastline, though, is largely still in the hands of nature, and is still being shaped by erosion and the power of the sea.

Towns such as Weymouth and Poole have grown up around shipping and fishing, their seamen going out to brave the rough tides and wild seas of the English Channel. Portland and Purbeck, both really peninsulas, not islands, bear the marks of the quarrymen who have wrought out tons of stone, not only for local buildings but for distant landmarks such as St Paul's Cathedral. Yet these parts of Dorset bear their scars proudly, like battle honours rather than as a despoliation.

Despite the occasional intrusion of a holiday camp or caravan park, the coast remains unspoiled between the major towns. Waves still crash on the long and lonely shingle of Chesil Beach, just as J Meade Faulkner described it in his Victorian smuggling romance 'Moonfleet'. Beyond this huge ridge of stones is the Fleet itself, that strange lake of brackish water that begins at Abbotsbury, where it is white with swans, to its end against the narrow isthmus where the Isle of Portland meets the mainland.

Unlike neighbouring Devon, there are no great estuaries on this coastline, though the wide expanse of Poole Harbour gives welcome shelter to yachts. The harbours at Lyme Regis and West Bay are artificial constructions, won back from the sea to facilitate trade and the safety of shipping. Fishing villages such as Studland cling to the coast; below them are the beaches of sand and shingle where fishing families have launched their boats from generation to generation.

Weymouth and Poole are still important ports, and have become resorts by mere fluke. Bournemouth, on the other hand, was almost purposely built to cater for tourists, from Lewis Tregonwell, who built the first holiday home there in 1810, to the tourist flats and hotels of today. This huge town has now dwarfed its ancient neighbour Christchurch. But both Bournemouth and Christchurch are really cuckoos in the nest, belonging still in spirit, as they once did in actuality, to neighbouring Hampshire.

Each coastal town has charm and individuality; it would be difficult to confuse one with any other, so much are they distinct in character and style. They are a taste of Dorset at its best, and the discerning visitor will savour the chance to linger and explore.

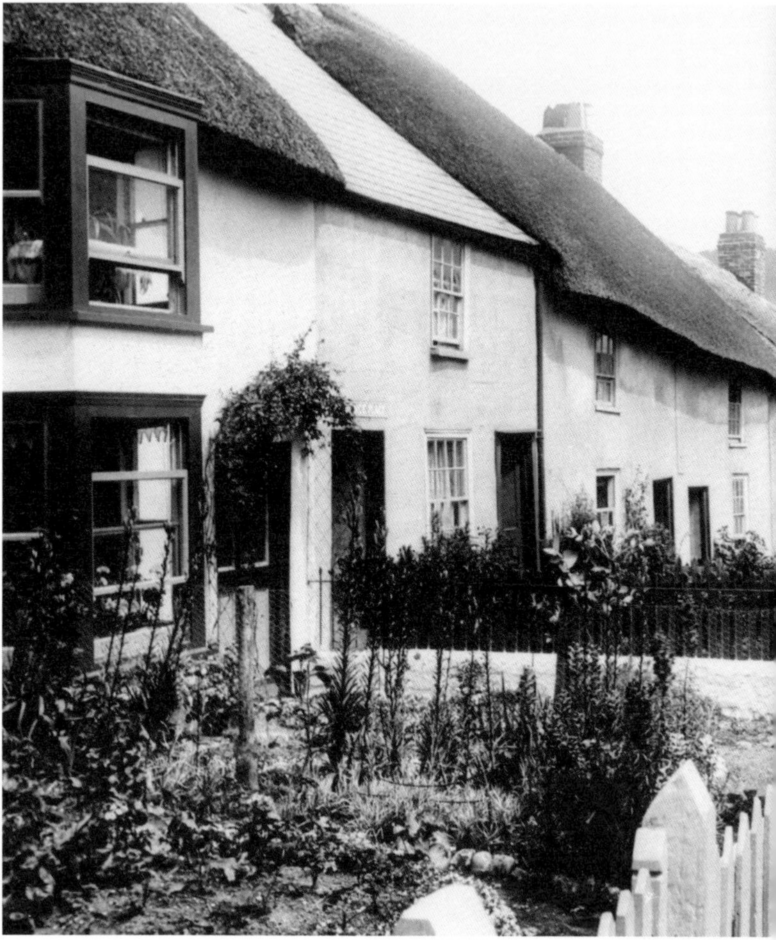

LYME REGIS

SHERBORNE LANE 1907 / 58099

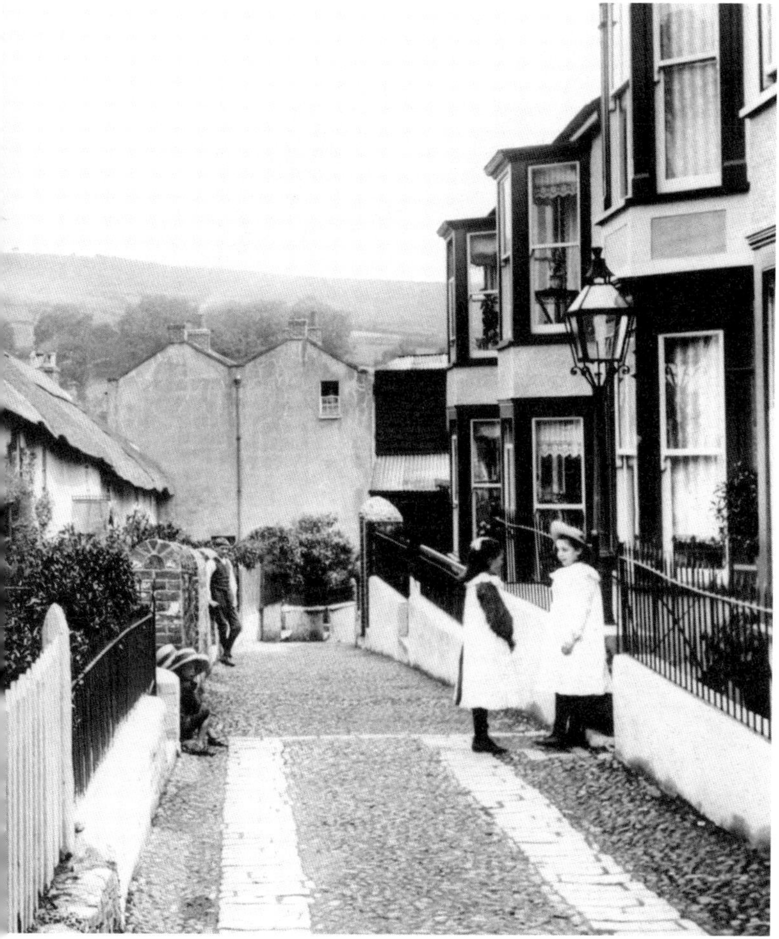

Sherborne Lane is shown here when the Crown and Anchor, the large building at the foot of the hill, was still open. This is probably the oldest part of Lyme, being built on land given to Sherborne Abbey in 744 by King Cynewulf, King of Wessex.

Lyme Regis features a great deal in English literature, being the setting of Jane Austen's novel 'Persuasion' and John Fowles's 'The French Lieutenant's Woman'. Few who saw the film version of the latter will forget the scene where the enigmatic heroine, played by Meryl Streep, stood braving a storm at the end of the Cobb—Lyme's harbour wall.

LYME REGIS

BROAD STREET 1900 / 45242

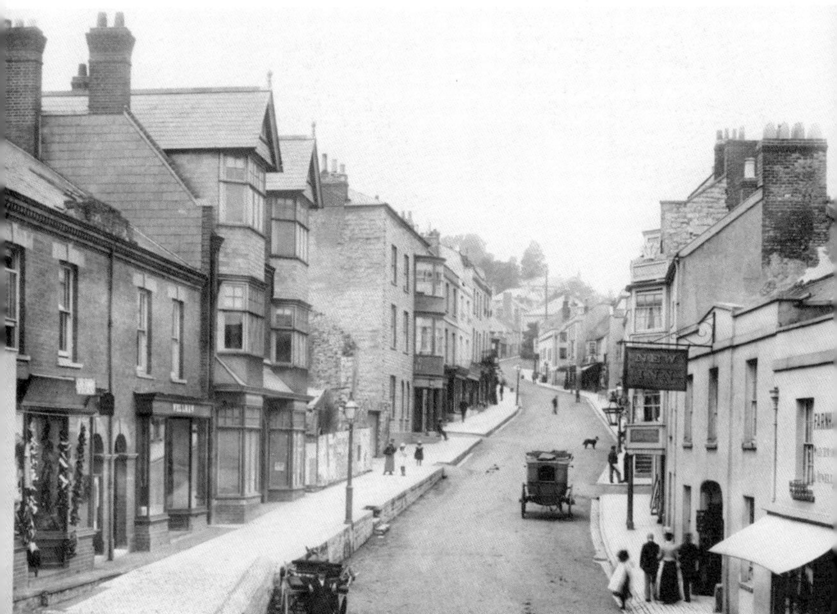

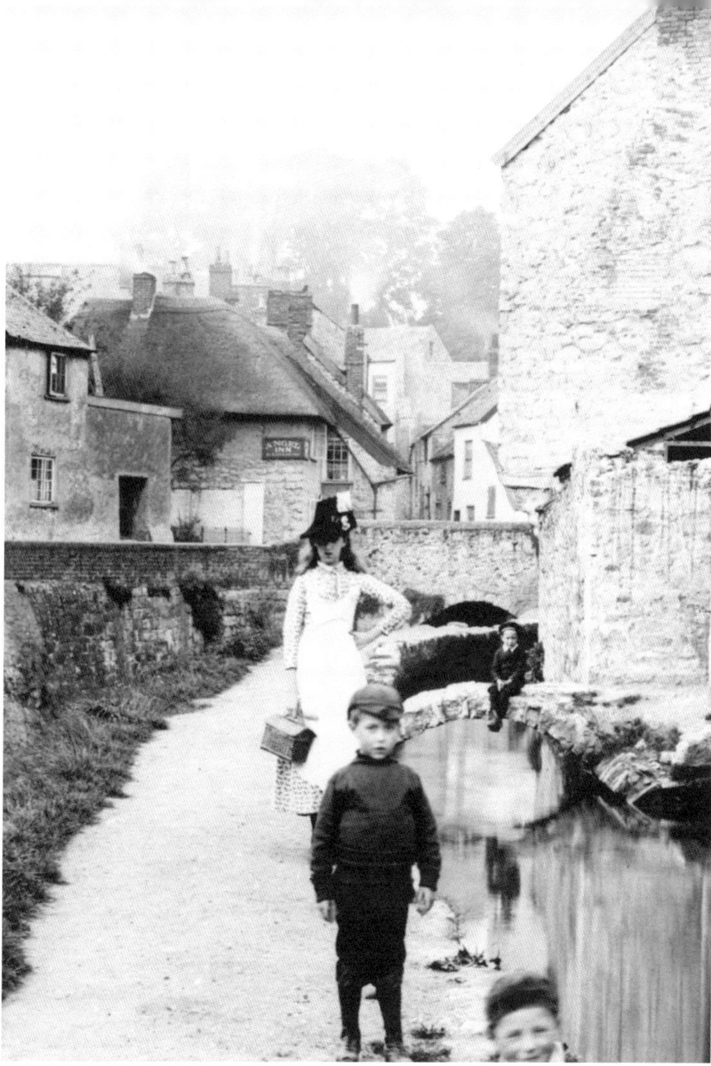

LYME REGIS

THE LYNCH 1892 / 31311

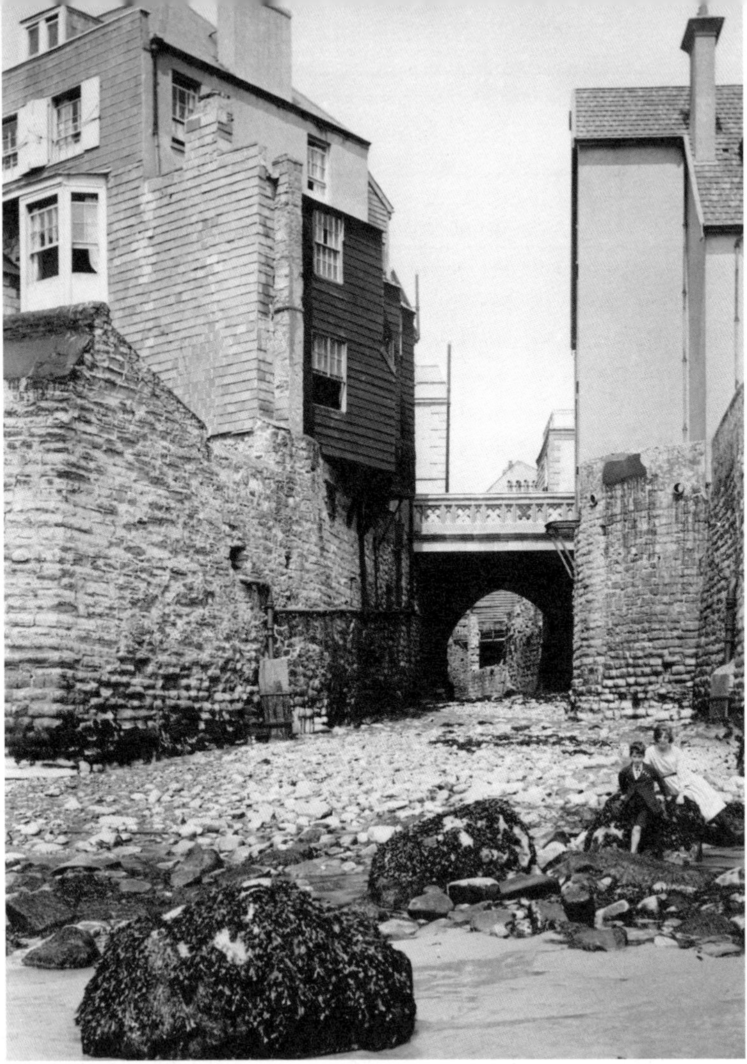

LYME REGIS

BUDDLE BRIDGE 1922 / 72770

Lyme Regis was relatively late in having the advantage of its own railway line, for its station opened only in 1903. Cannington Viaduct, near Uplyme, was one of the first railway bridges to be made out of concrete. The railway link to the town was severed in the 1960s.

LYME REGIS

CANNINGTON VIADUCT 1903 / 50253

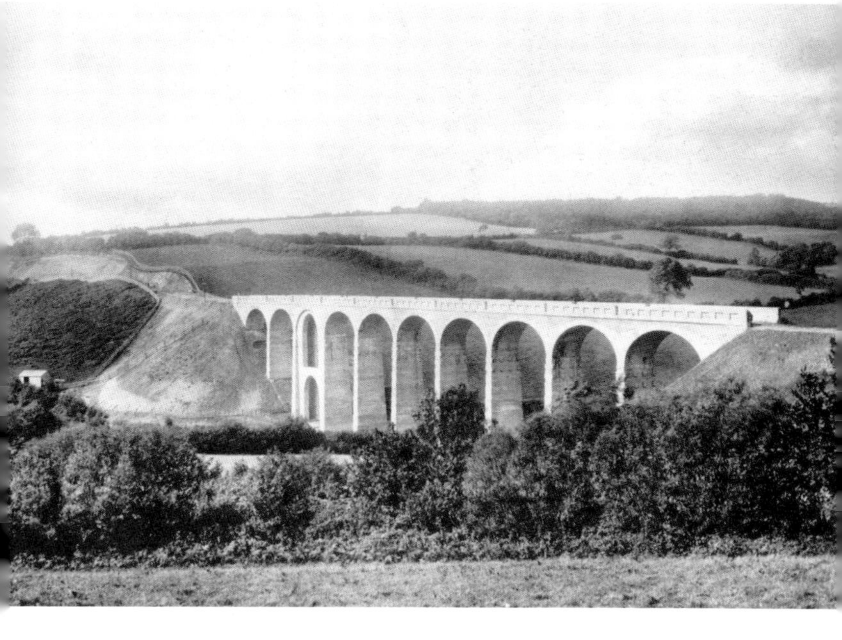

BURTON BRADSTOCK

THE VILLAGE 1902 / 48412

Henry I gave the village and living of Burton Bradstock to the great Normandy abbey at Caen in exchange for the royal regalia of William the Conqueror, which the monks claimed had been gifted to them by the dying king. This lovely village was considered a reasonable exchange for England's crown jewels.

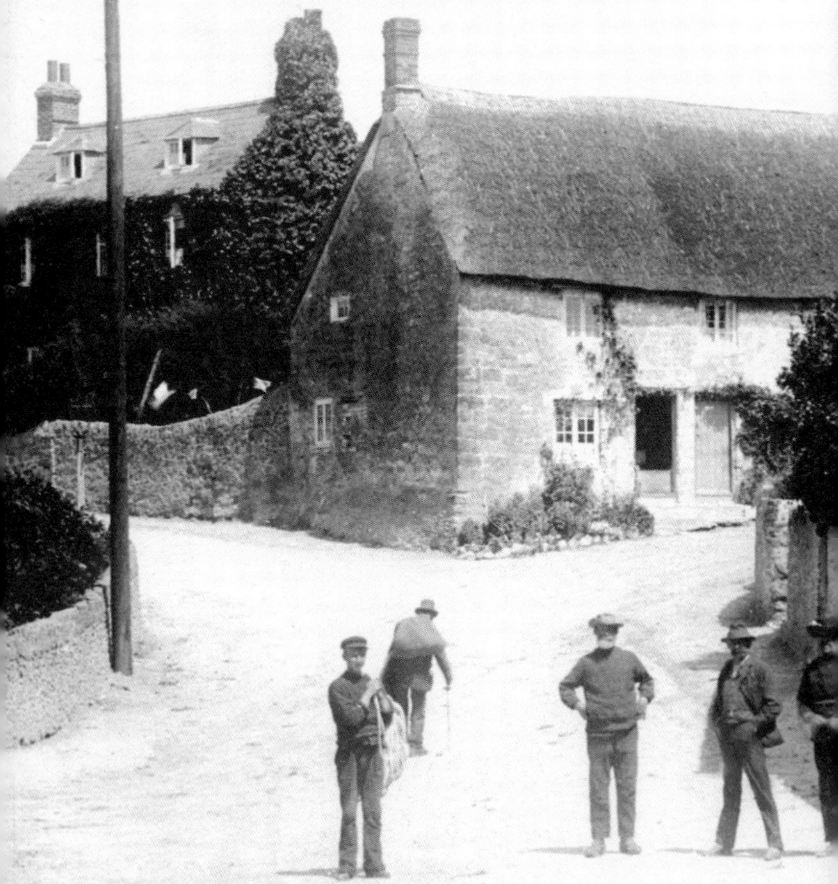

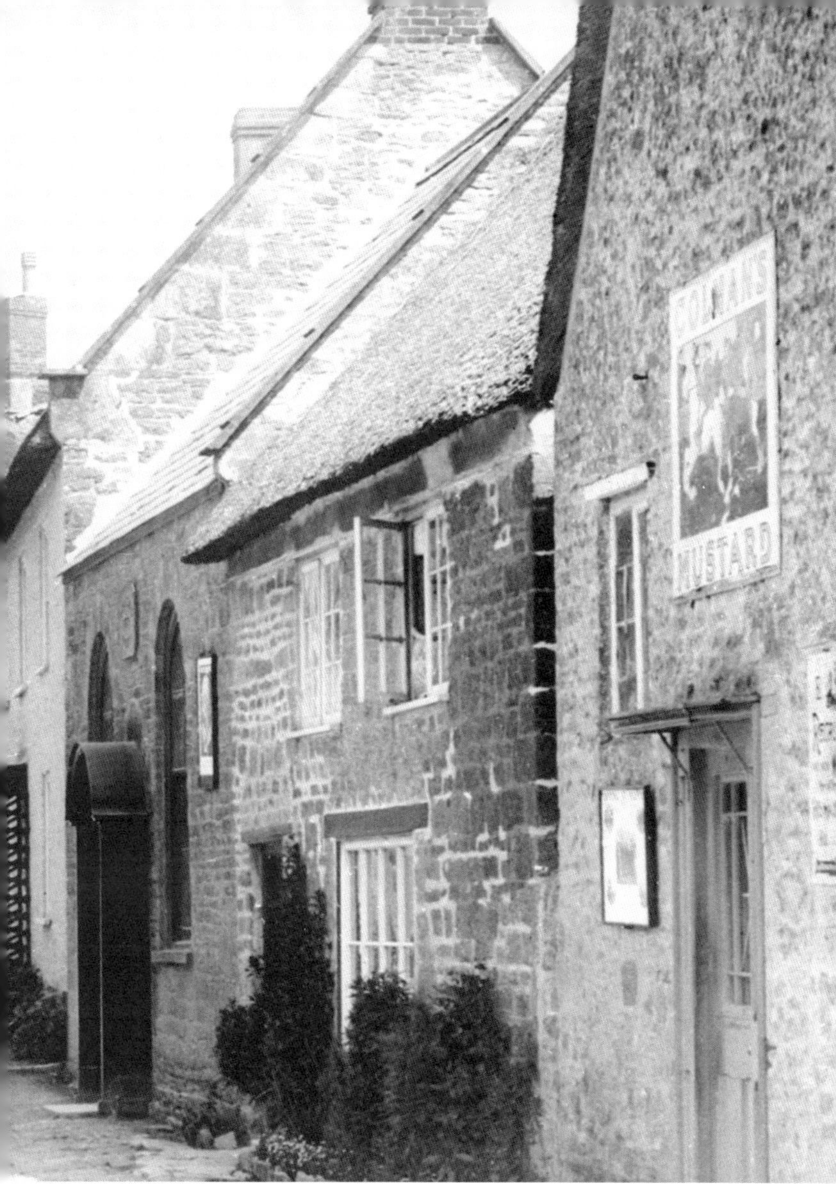
MUSTARD

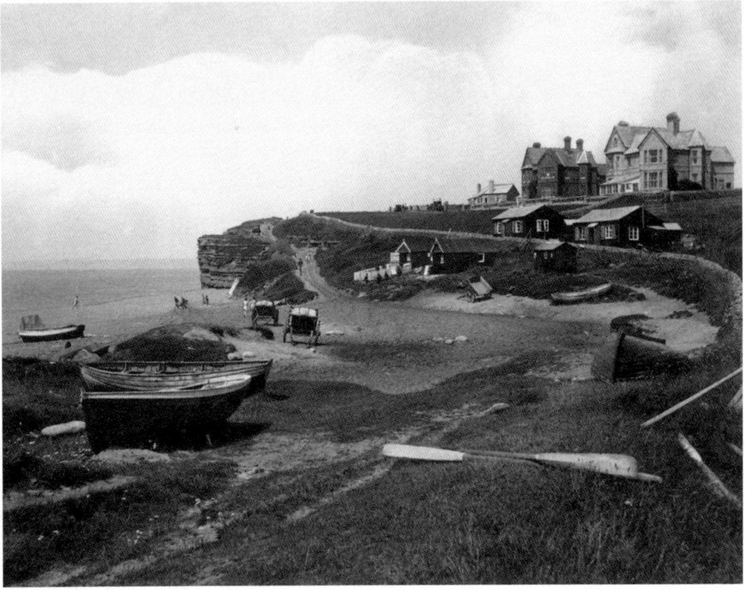

Such is the unbroken nature of the West Dorset coastline that artificial harbours had to be constructed at Lyme Regis and West Bay. The small coves between, such as the beach below Burton Bradstock, would be used mostly by local fishermen and smugglers.

BURTON BRADSTOCK

THE BEACH 1930 / 83366

CHIDEOCK

THE VILLAGE 1912 / 65080

Chideock, always pronounced without the 'e', is set in a landscape of ancient ridgeways and rolling hills. Its charming cottages witnessed some of the fiercest fighting of the English Civil War, and its narrow streets some of the most daring smuggling escapades of recent centuries.

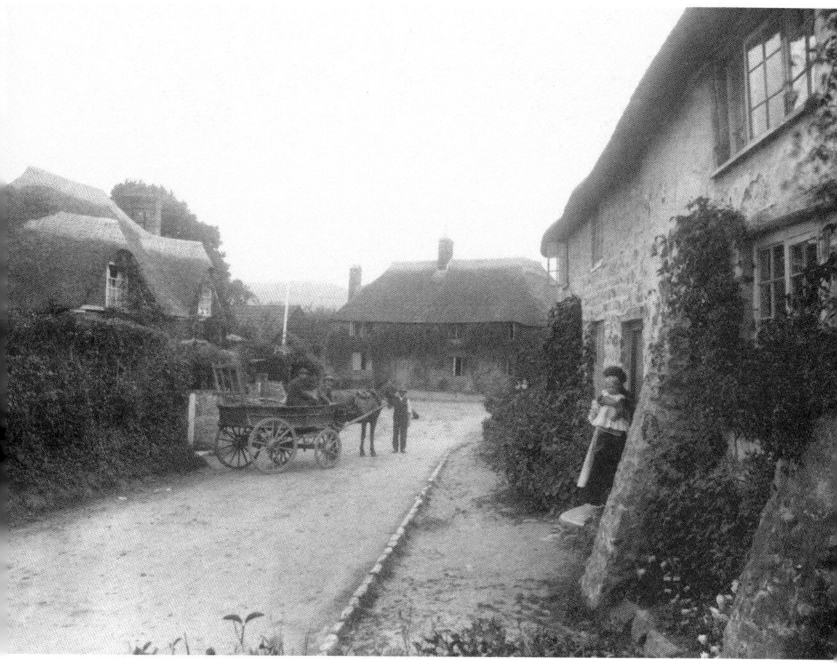

Abbotsbury, situated at the western end of Chesil Beach, is most famous for its swannery, the waters of the Fleet often being turned white with hundreds of birds. But for centuries the village was the location of a substantial monastery. Only a few ruins and the tithe barn remain.

ABBOTSBURY

THE TITHE BARN 1890 / 27322

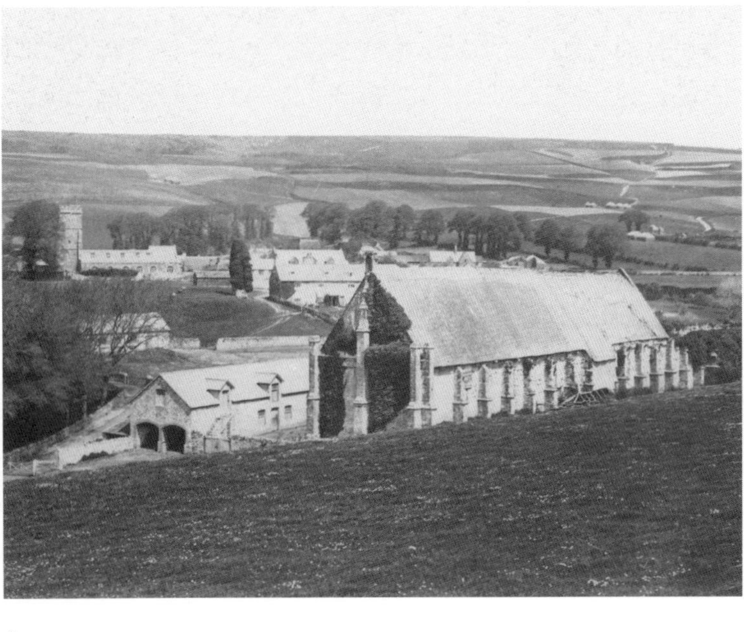

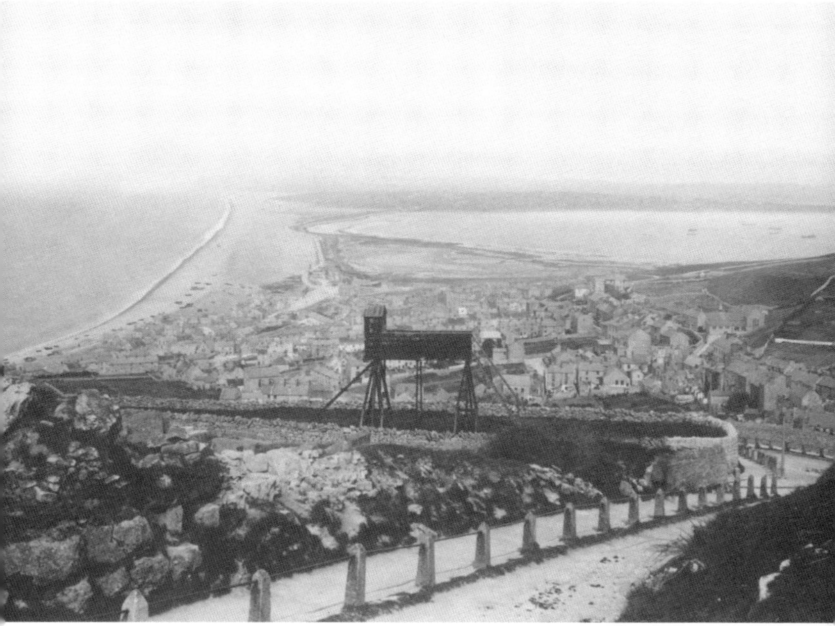

Chesil Beach, seen here from the Isle of Portland, is a great ridge of shingle eight miles long, with a lagoon of brackish water between it and the mainland. Its stones tend to be much larger at one end than the other. John Meade Faulkner immortalised the area in his famous smuggling novel 'Moonfleet'.

PORTLAND

CHESIL BEACH 1890 / 27328

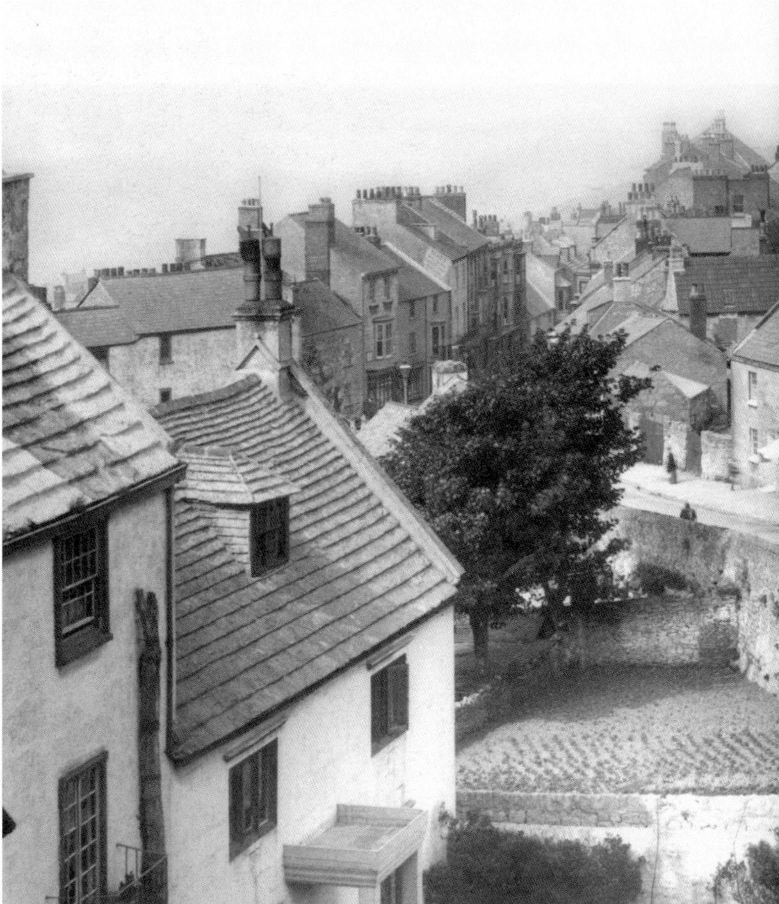

PORTLAND

FORTUNESWELL 1894 / 34550

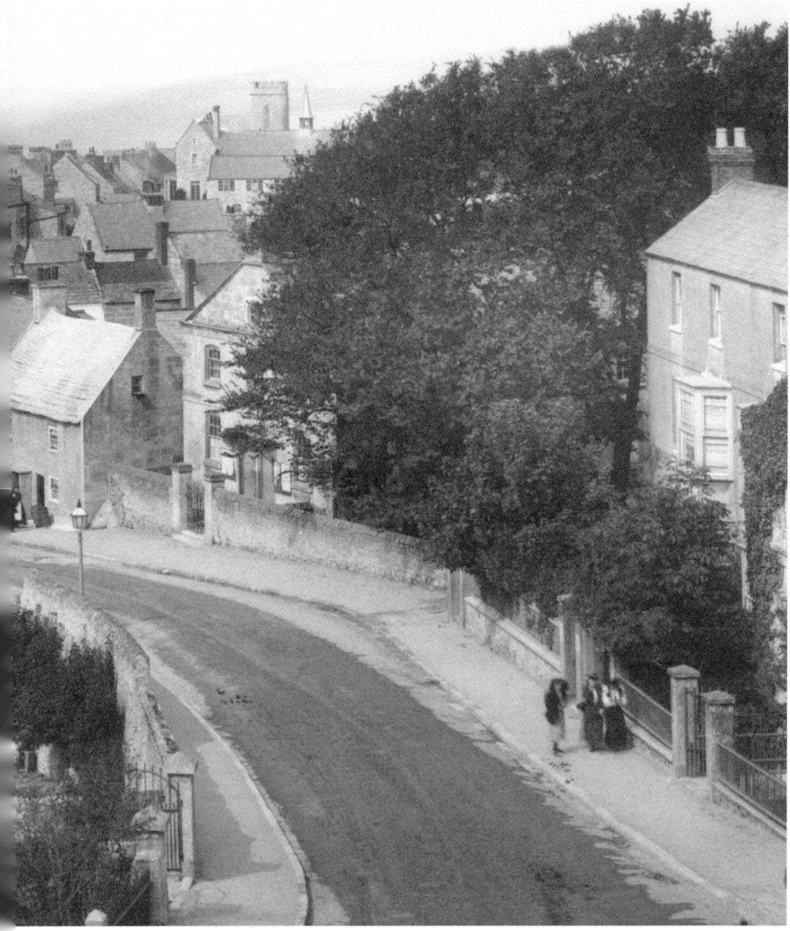

The Isle's main town of Fortuneswell grew up, as the name implies, around a supply of fresh water, as did many of the Portland settlements. On this barren rock, surrounded by salt water, such wells were hard to come by and exploited to the full when they were.

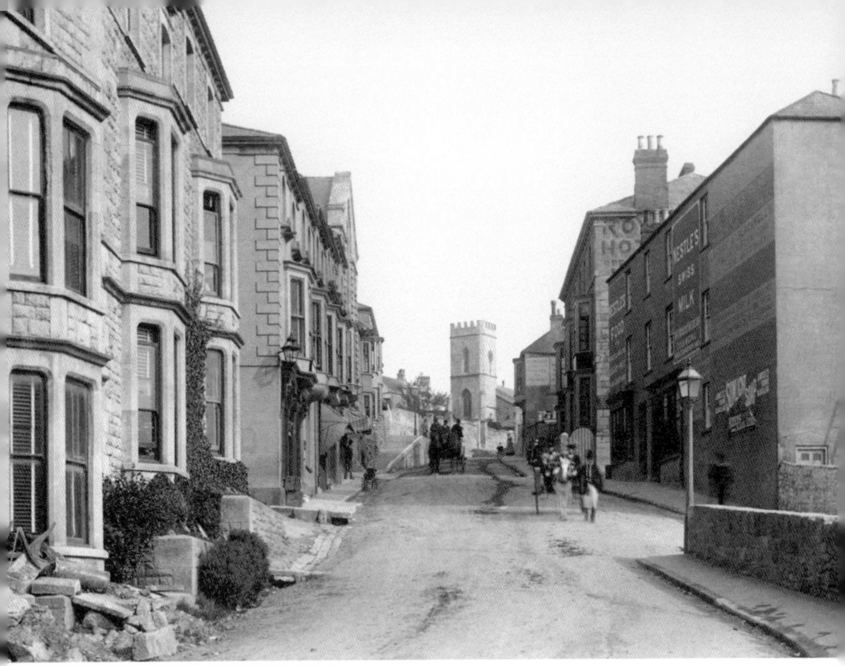

The Portland villages of Castleton, Fortuneswell and Chesil now form the largest urban settlement where the Isle meets the causeway from the mainland. When this photograph was taken, they were three discreet villages, overlooking the great naval base in one direction and being overlooked by the convict prison from the other.

PORTLAND

STREET SCENE 1894 / 34551

Sandsfoot Castle, now tumbling into the sea, was built by Henry VIII to guard the sea-lanes between Weymouth and Portland. The Tudor topographer Leland described it as being 'a right goodlie and warlyke castle'. It changed hands several times during the Civil War, before finally falling into ruin in the 1700s.

WEYMOUTH

SANDSFOOT CASTLE 1898 / 41138

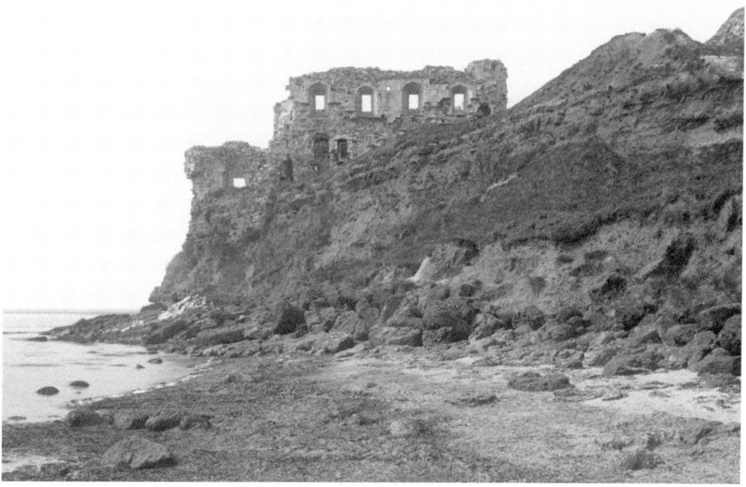

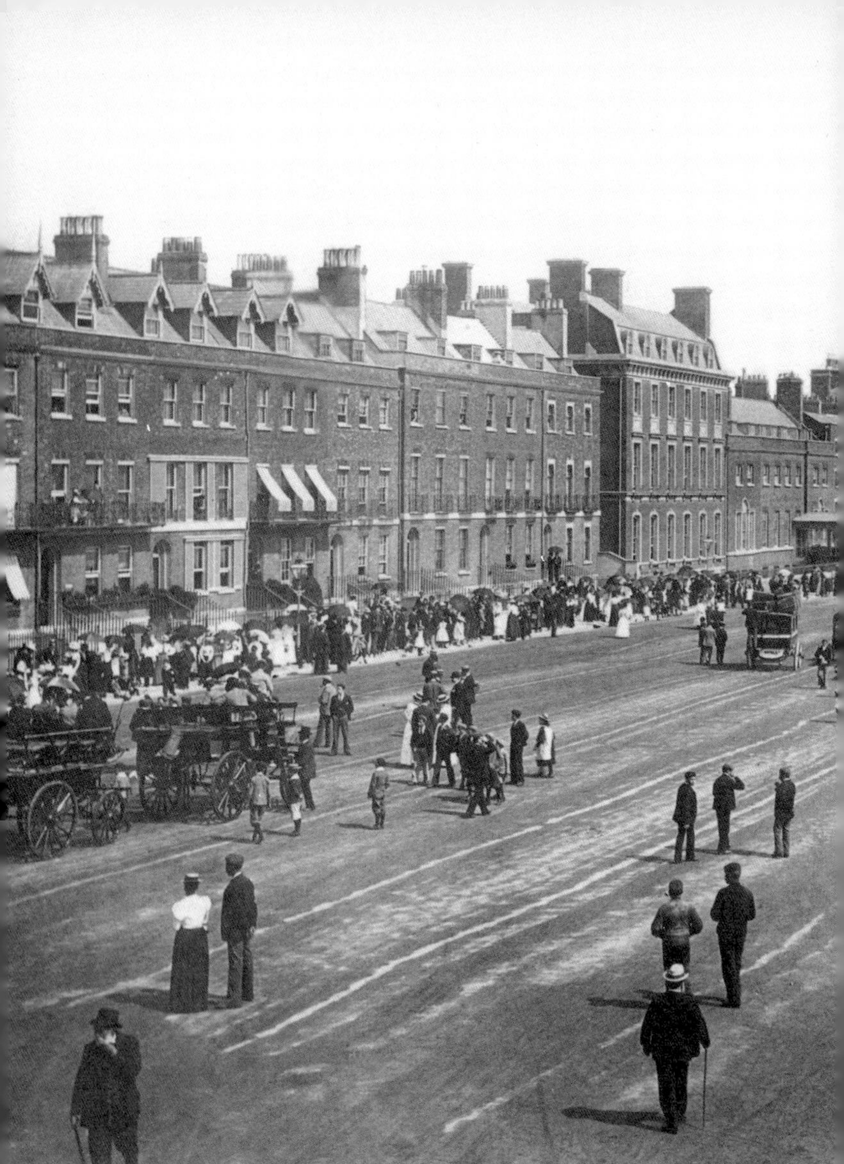

WEYMOUTH

THE ESPLANADE 1899 / 43852

Weymouth became popular as a seaside resort thanks to the patronage of George III, who came to bathe here for the good of his health. As the king plunged into the waves a brass band, discreetly hidden in a bathing machine, played God Save the King!

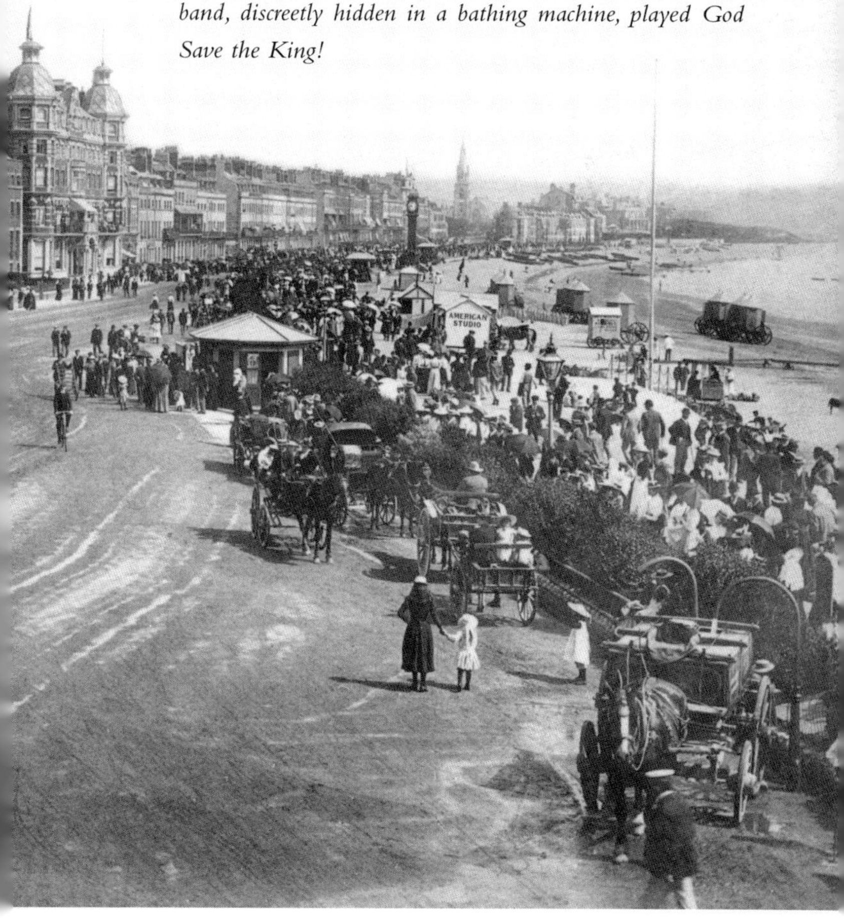

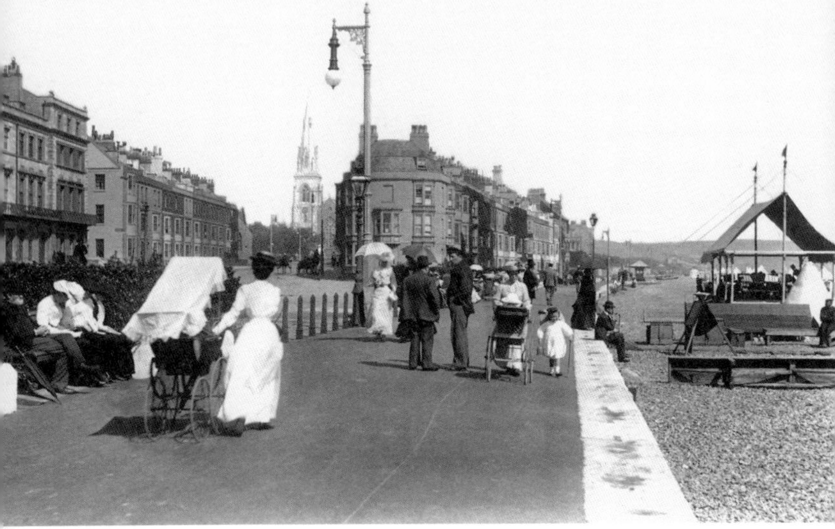

An old guidebook stressed the benefits to health of a holiday in Weymouth: 'Weymouth is much more open than the majority of seaside resorts, and is almost surrounded by salt water. This results in an air largely impregnated with ozone and, with the ever-changing tide, ensures a constantly renewed atmosphere'.

WEYMOUTH

THE PARADE 1904 / 52858

The Pavilion Theatre was a year old when this photograph was taken. The new entertainment venue quickly eclipsed the other small halls around the town, offering a variety of plays all the year round to an audience of up to 1,100 people.

WEYMOUTH

THE PAVILION 1909 / 61594

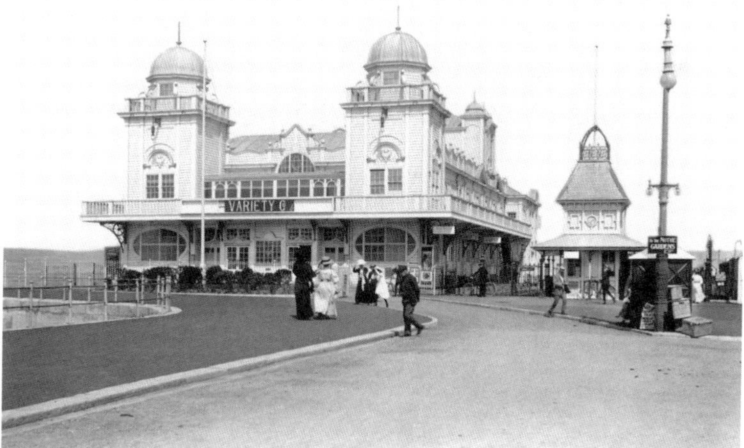

WEYMOUTH

THE PIER AND THE PAVILION 1909 / 61589

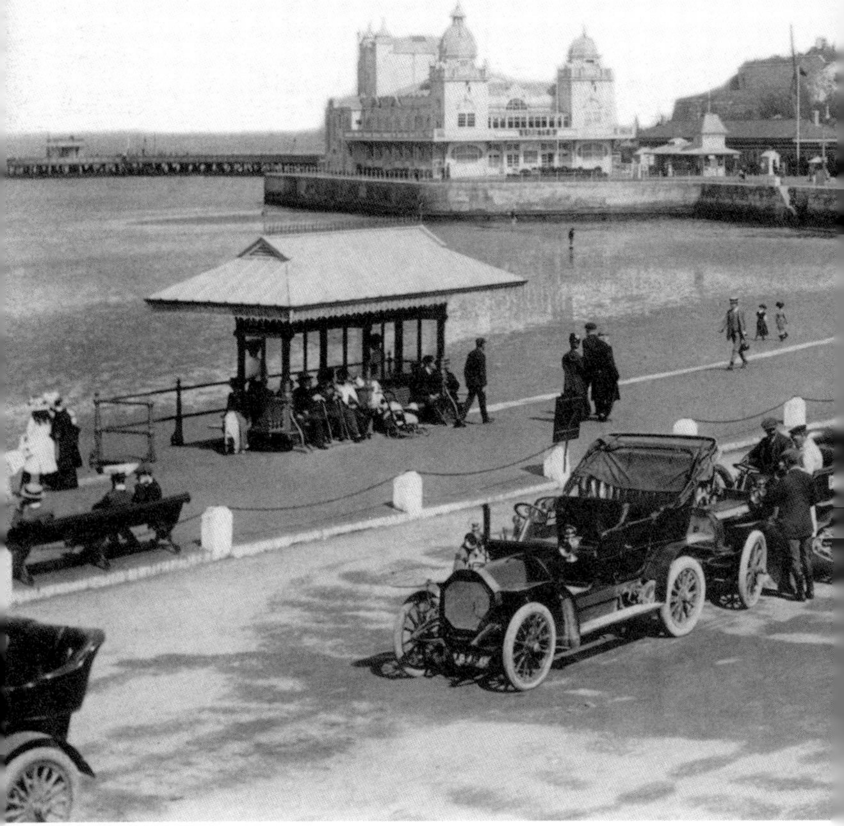

Weymouth esplanade winds round to the pier and pavilion theatre, a favourite stroll for the Edwardian visitors seen here. The pier at this time was 1050 feet long, and was a favoured location for watching the steamers come in and out. In 1909 the admission fee for the pier was 2d.

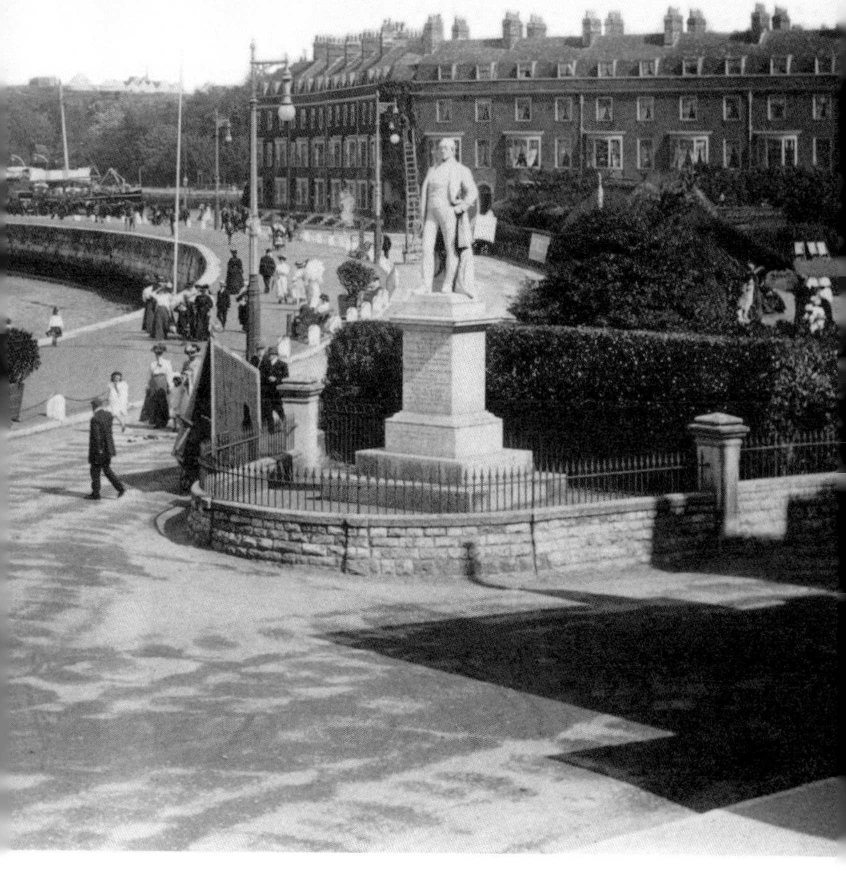

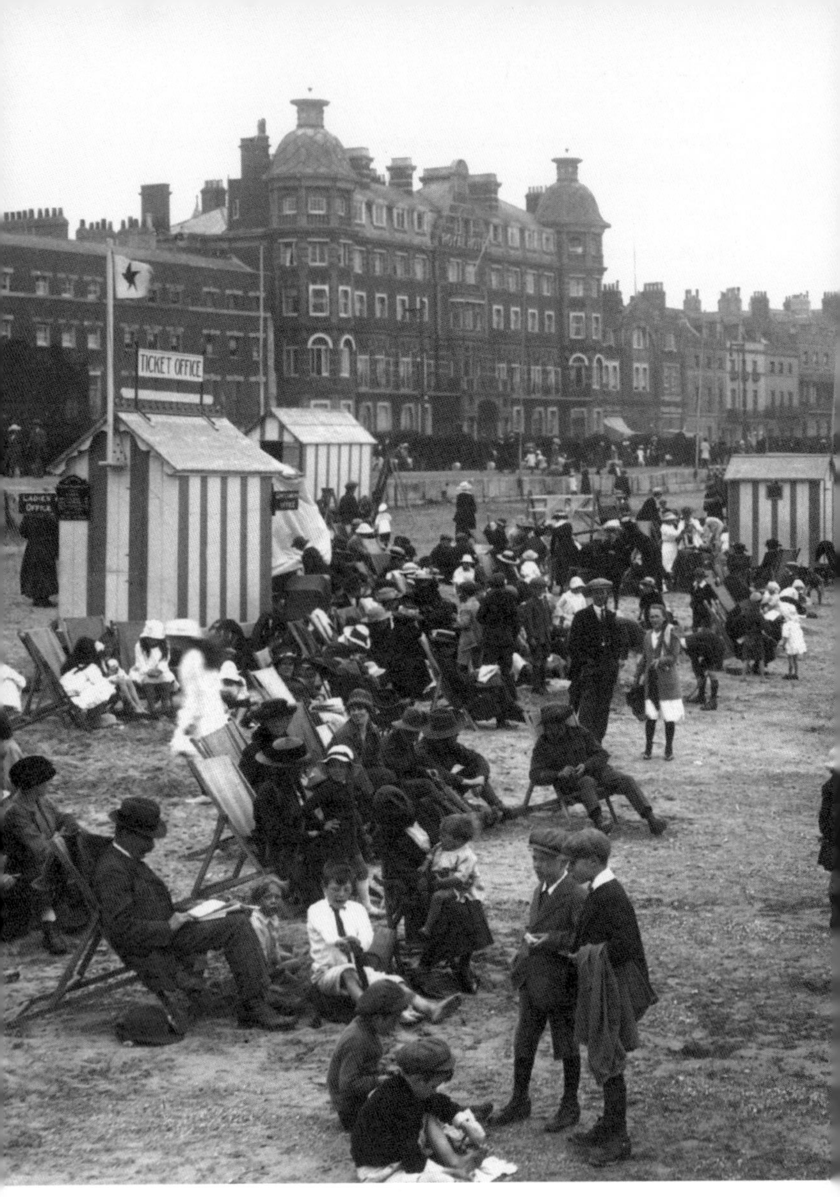
TICKET OFFICE

WEYMOUTH

THE SANDS 1918 / 68116

It was the early use of bathing machines that made Weymouth such a popular resort for sea bathing. The larger machines shown here ran down to the water on rails, and had a number of cubicles. Affluent visitors would hire single-cubicle machines for themselves.

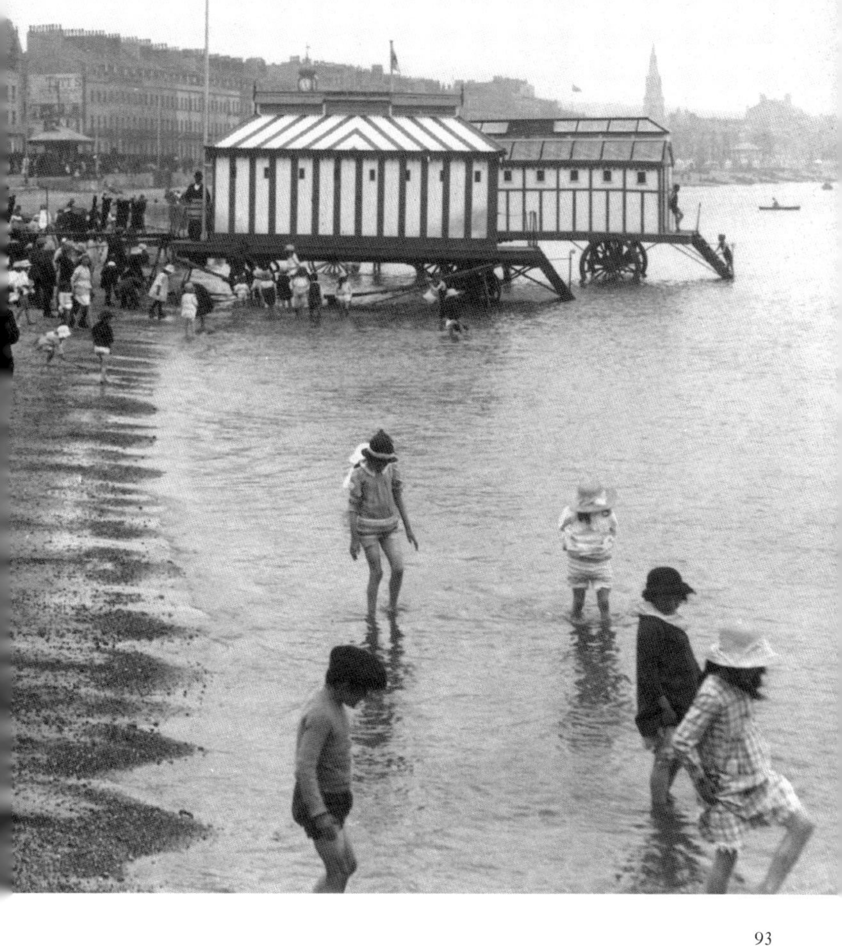

The great natural arch of Durdle Door braves the sea just a little way from the more famous Lulworth Cove. The beautiful surrounding coastline is lonely and unspoiled once the roads and traffic are left behind.

LULWORTH

DURDLE DOOR 1894 / 34583

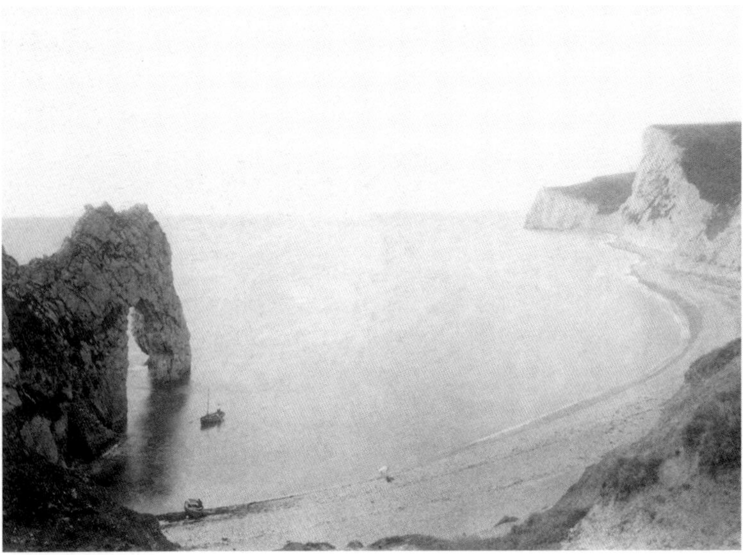

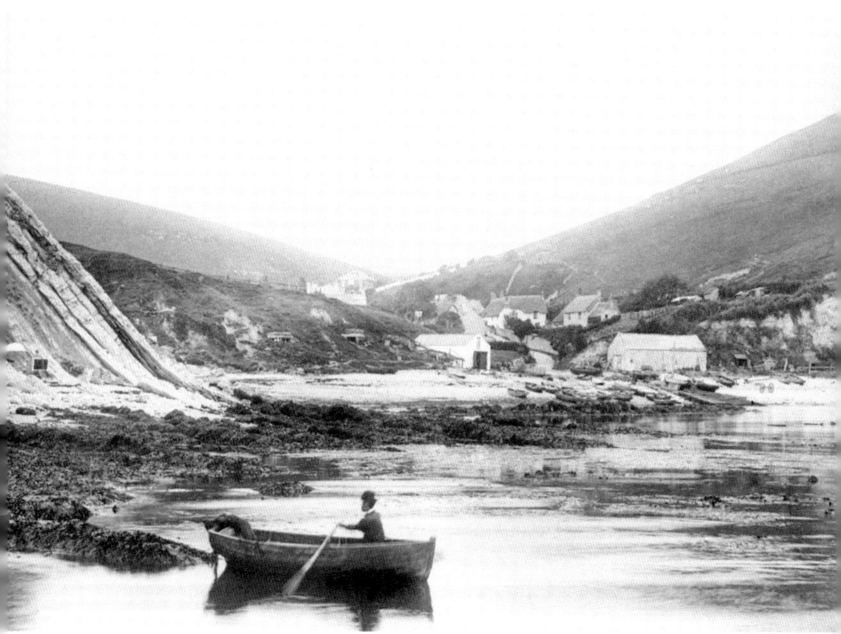

To the left, an artist sits at an easel and paints Lulworth Cove, while his wife shades herself with a parasol. By the end of the 19th century, the cove was already attracting a great many visitors. Its perfect natural harbour, hollowed out by the Channel into its present near-circular form, is one of the most distinctive bays on the English coastline.

LULWORTH

THE COVE 1894 / 34569

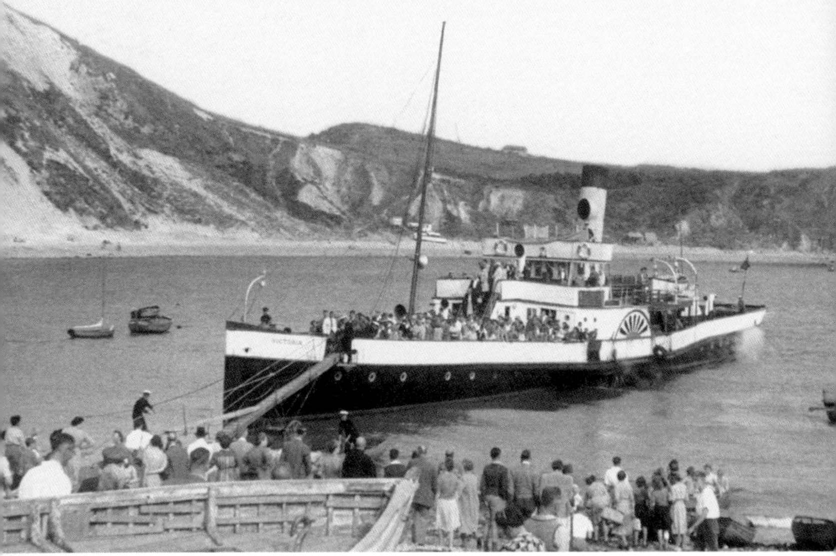

The beauty of Lulworth Cove has always attracted writers and artists. John Keats spent some of his last days in England here, as did Rupert Brooke. Thomas Hardy immortalised the cove in novels and poems, while artistic views are on sale in every Dorset gallery and gift shop.

LULWORTH

THE BEACH AND A STEAM BOAT C1955 / L112021

Thomas Hardy described Swanage as '...a seaside village, lying snugly within two headlands as between a finger and thumb'. The town may get its name from Swene's Wic, the Bay of Swene, perhaps commemorating the great naval battle fought nearby between the Saxons and Danes in 877.

SWANAGE

THE BEACH 1899 / 43762

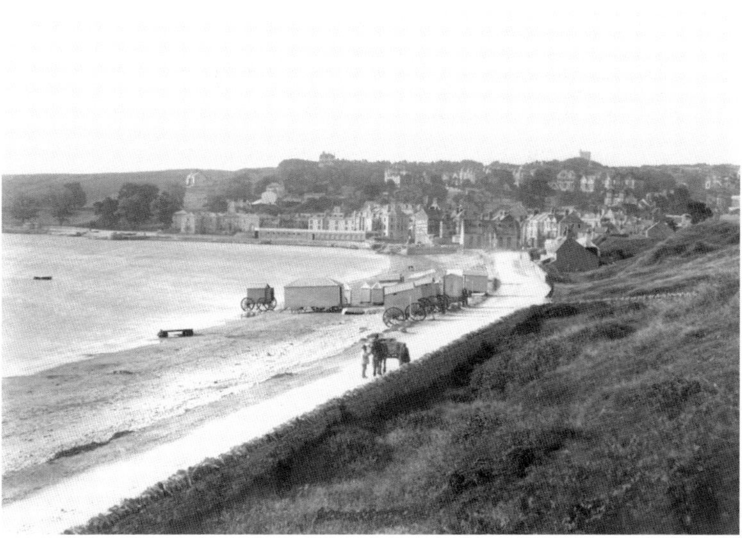

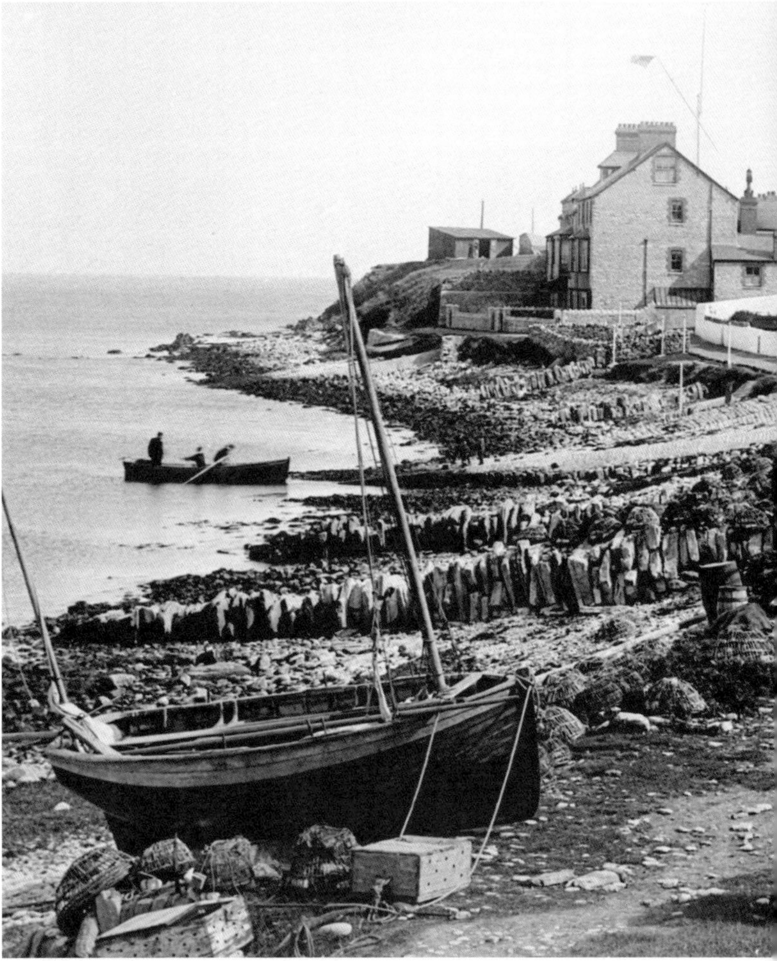

SWANAGE

THE COASTGUARD STATION 1897 / 40310

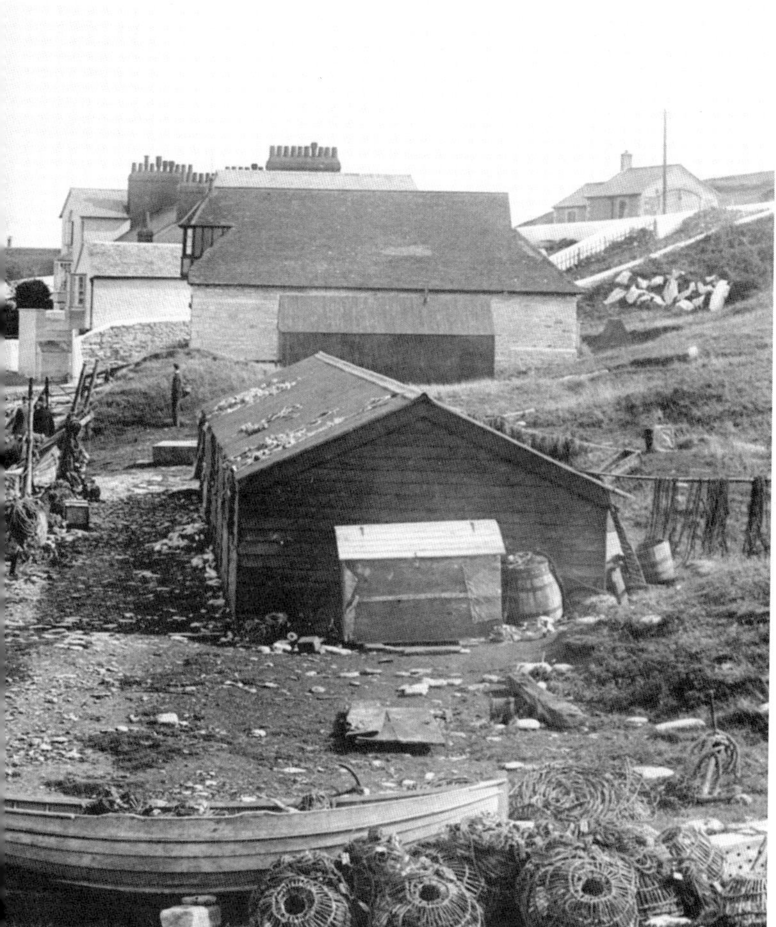

For hundreds of years smuggling was a major industry in Swanage: the smuggled goods were hidden in the local caves and quarries. Prominent coastguard stations were built along the coast to act as a deterrent.

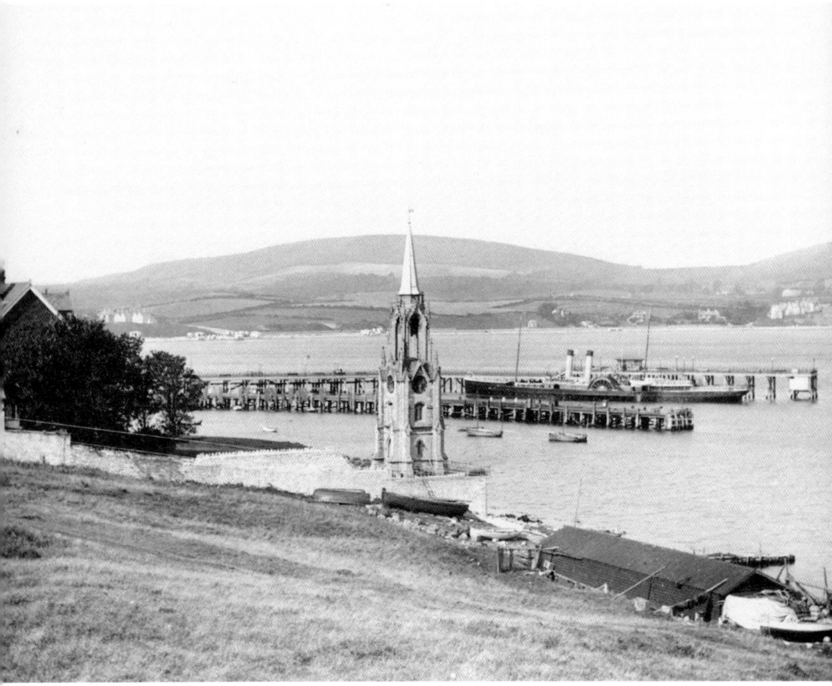

Swanage pier is really a jetty, 28 feet wide and 1,400 feet long. In 1897 the pier would have been used either to give access to the many passenger steamers that plied their trade along the coast or to transport the famous Purbeck stone on merchant ships.

SWANAGE

FROM THE COASTGUARD STATION 1897 / 40308

Carriages are drawn up on the approach to the pier to collect passengers from the arriving steamers. Elsewhere, strollers pay their pennies to come through the turnstile to walk the pier and sample the balmy sea air.

SWANAGE

FROM THE PIER 1897 / 40305

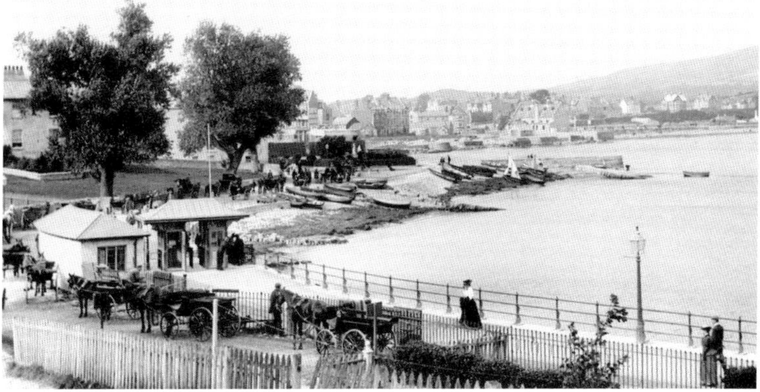

Studland's most famous resident was Sergeant William Lawrence, who fought with Wellington in Spain and at Waterloo. He spent his retirement running the village inn with his French wife Clothilde. Both now rest in the churchyard.

STUDLAND

THE NEW INN 1890 / 25557

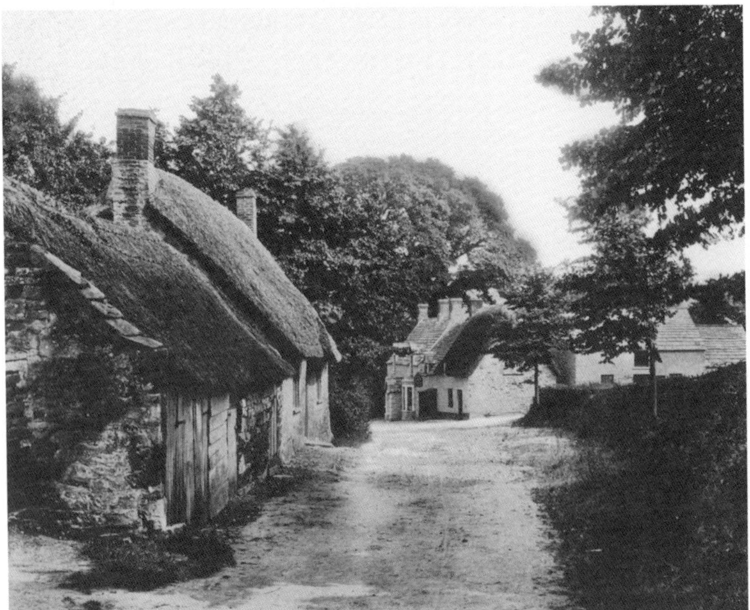

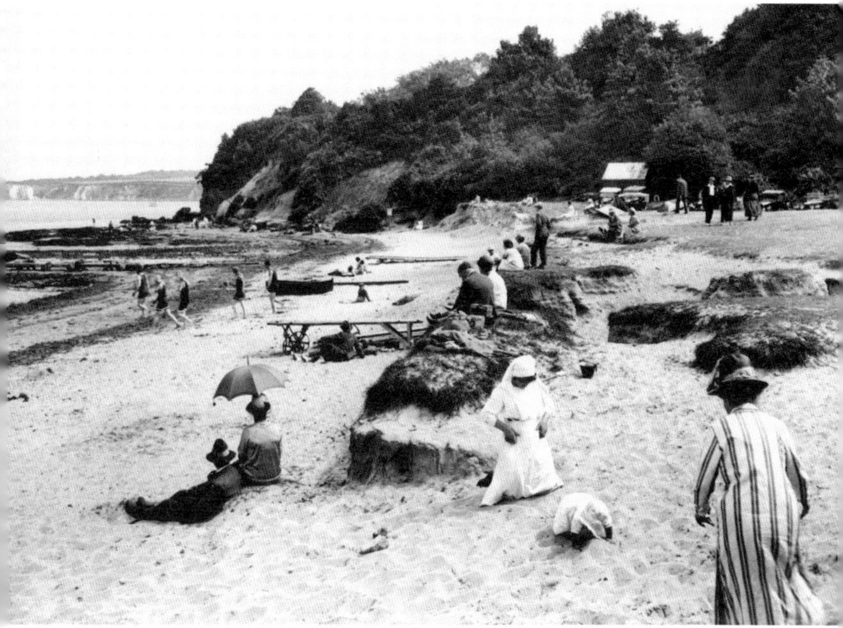

The attraction of Studland is not only the attractive beach and picturesque coastal scenery, but also the wild heathland around the village. Studland Heath is now a national nature reserve, famous for the variety of its birdlife.

STUDLAND

THE BEACH 1925 / 78796

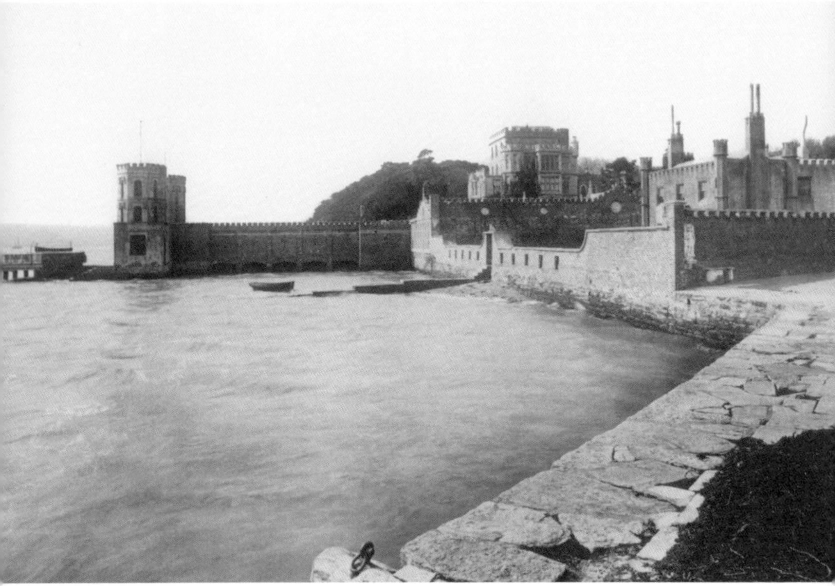

Brownsea is the largest island in Poole Harbour, and now belongs to the National Trust. In 1907, Robert Baden Powell held a camp for boys on the island, which laid the foundations for the Boy Scout movement.

BROWNSEA ISLAND

THE CASTLE 1891 / 29621

Poole's Town Cellars, in the heart of Poole's mercantile district, are seen here on a busy day . The town had many independent breweries at this time; here we see one of their horse-drawn drays preparing for a delivery round.

POOLE

THE TOWN CELLARS 1887 / 19511

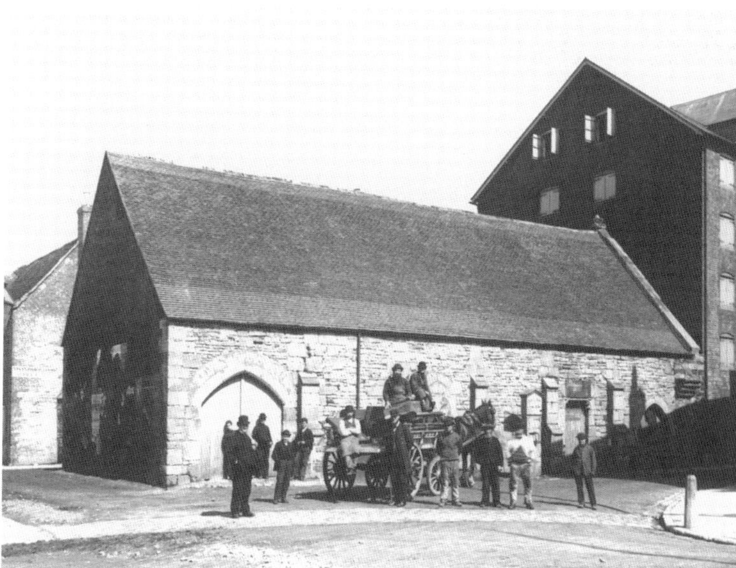

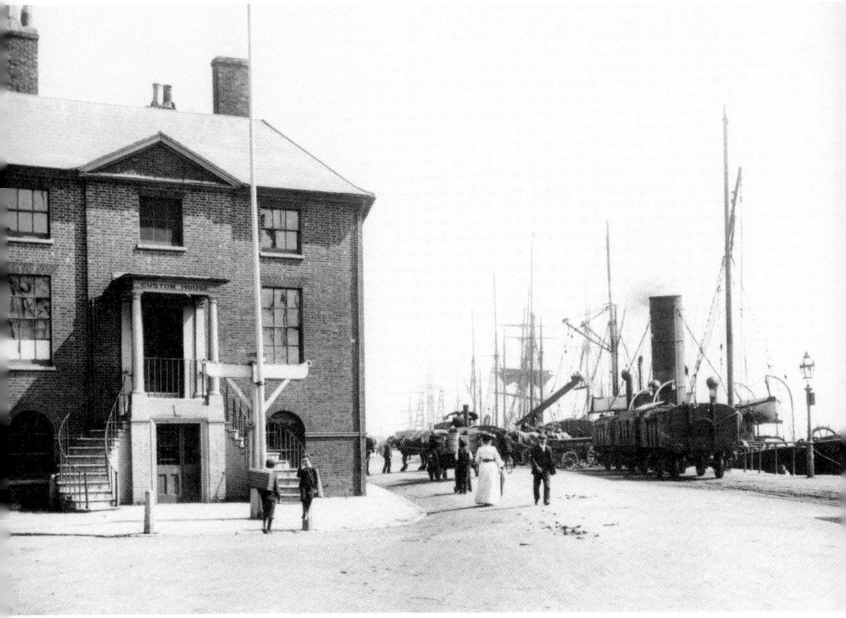

In 1747 a valuable cargo of tea was seized by the revenue men and stored in the Custom House at Poole. A band of well-armed smugglers attacked the building, stealing the tea and putting the revenue men to flight.

POOLE

THE CUSTOM HOUSE 1904 / 52814

Poole developed alongside the finest natural harbour in England; it still maintains strong links with the sea, having become a mecca for yachtsmen. The prosperous town, built where the sea meets the wild heathlands of Dorset, is one of the largest on England's south coast.

POOLE

HIGH STREET 1900 / 46088

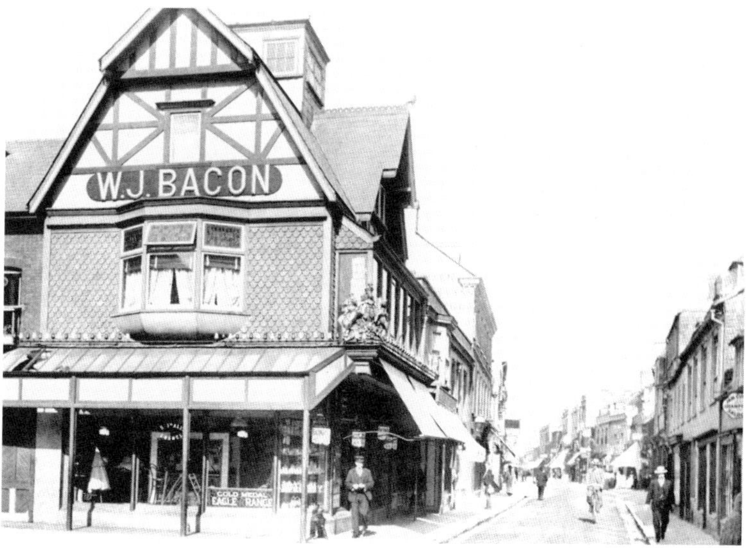

Poole did not become a holiday resort for many years, but retained its importance as a port and merchant centre. By 1904 holidaymakers were discovering the delights of the locality, and some of the sandier areas of Poole Harbour were attracting bathers.

POOLE

HIGH STREET 1904 / 52807

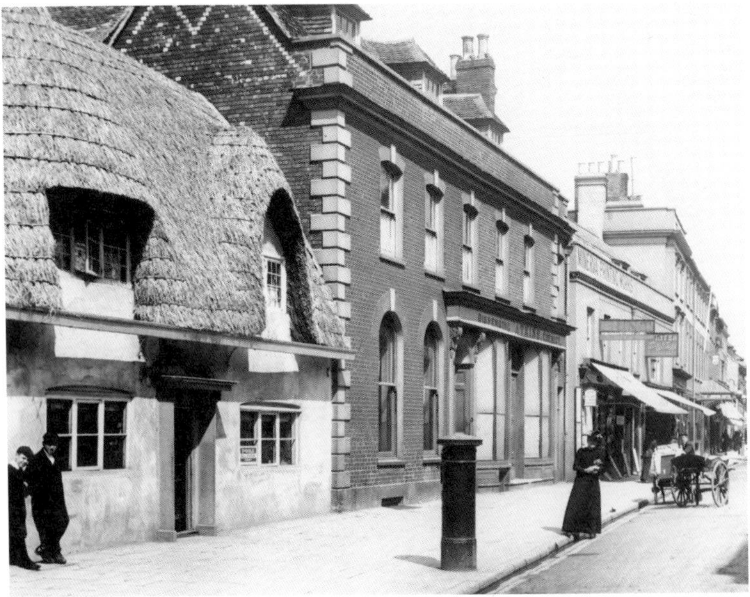

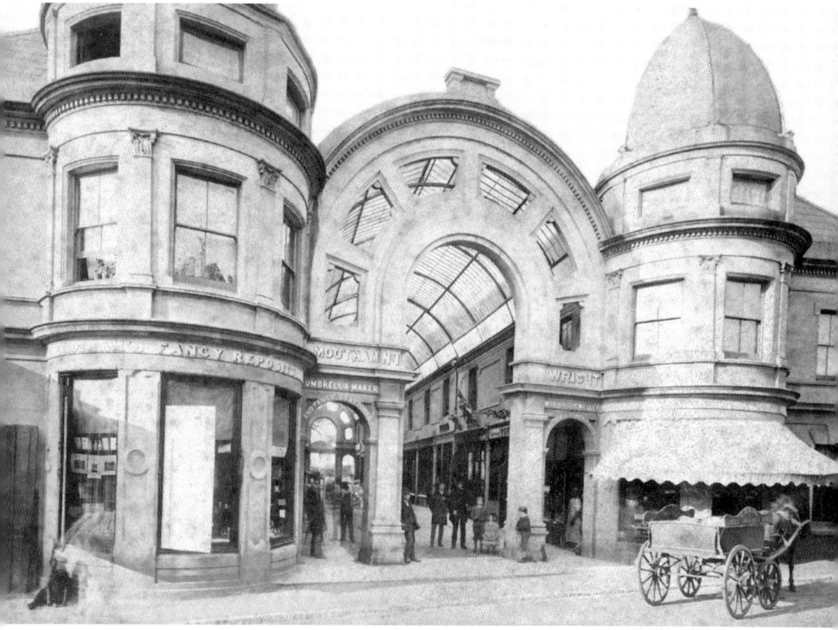

As with so many seaside resorts of the 19th century, Bournemouth attracted a wealthy and fashionable clientele. Shopkeepers were not long in seeing the business potential of catering for both residents and tourists. Shops and arcades were opened in the centre of town, such as the splendid example of Victorian architecture shown here.

BOURNEMOUTH

THE ARCADE C1871 / 5511

BOURNEMOUTH

FROM THE PIER 1897 / 40559

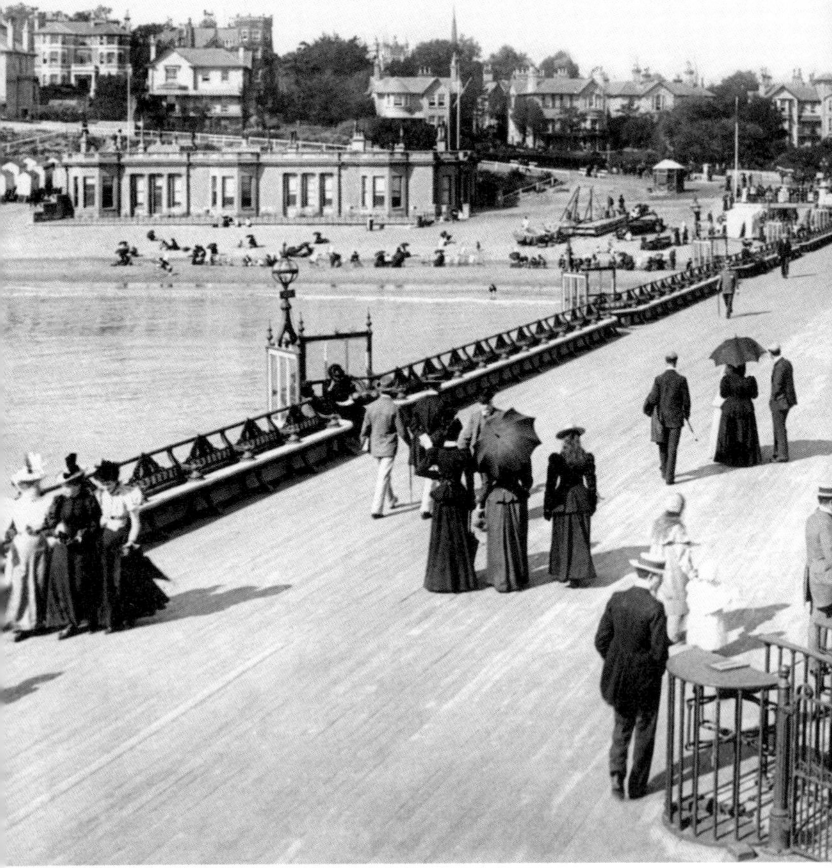

Less than a century after its foundation, the town was already dominating the skyline and its beaches were among the most crowded on the south coast. Thomas Hardy immortalised the town as 'the city of detached mansions' in 'Tess of the D'Urbervilles'.

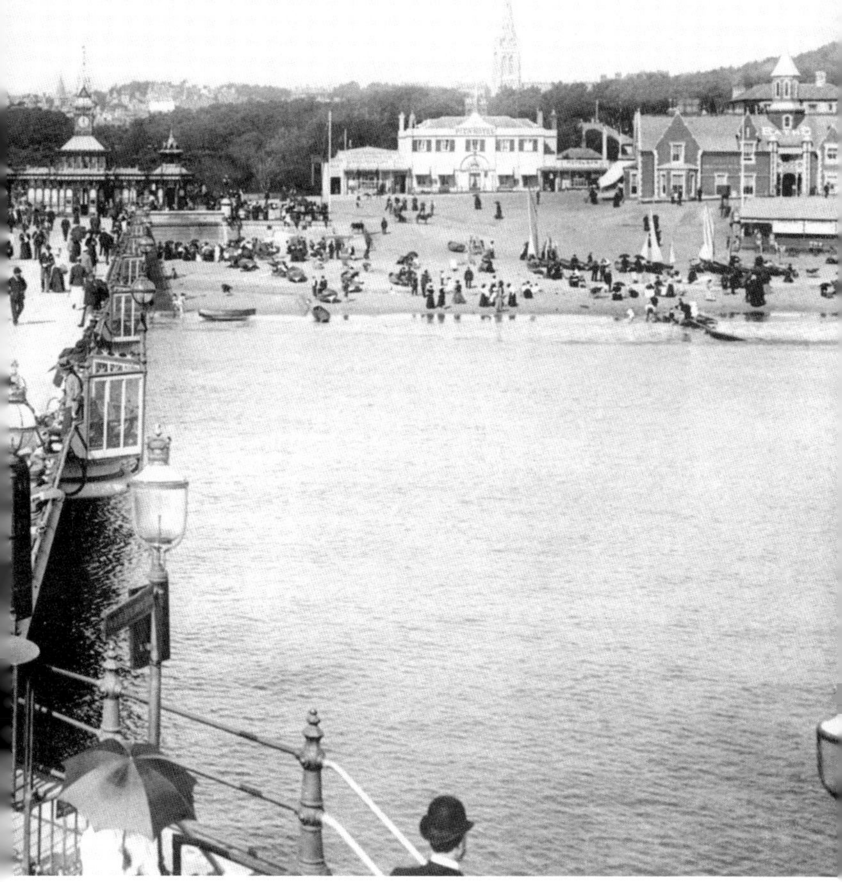

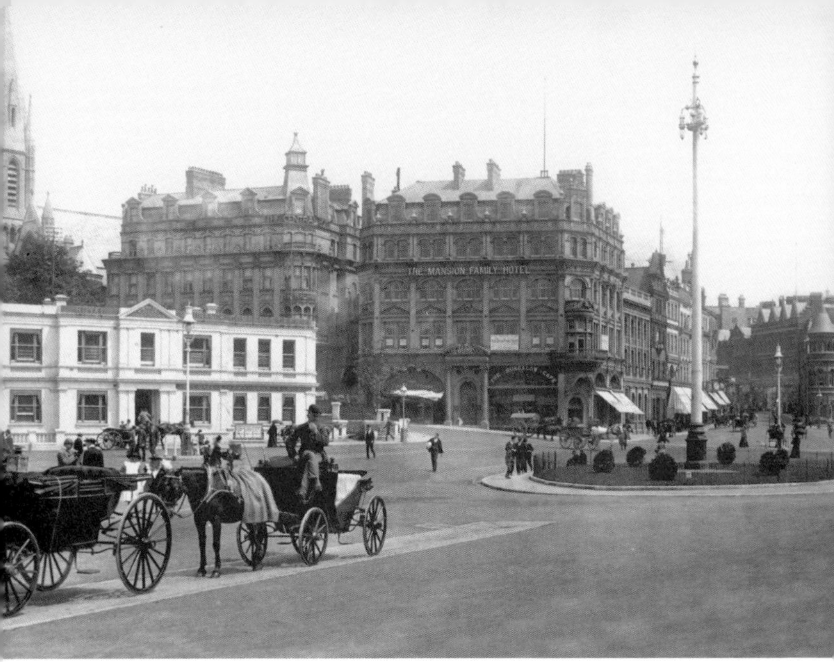

Bournemouth's Square stands at the very heart of the town astride the River Bourne. Here we see the carriages of the wealthy assembled and waiting to take their clients back to their hotels and villas.

BOURNEMOUTH

THE SQUARE 1900 / 45218

A view of busy Bournemouth pier, attracting strollers and sightseers. The pier has undergone several transformations since it was first built, but retains its popularity. By the 1920s cars had almost completely replaced horse-drawn carriages, and charabanc tours had become a popular feature of a seaside holiday.

BOURNEMOUTH

THE PIER ENTRANCE 1925 / 78768

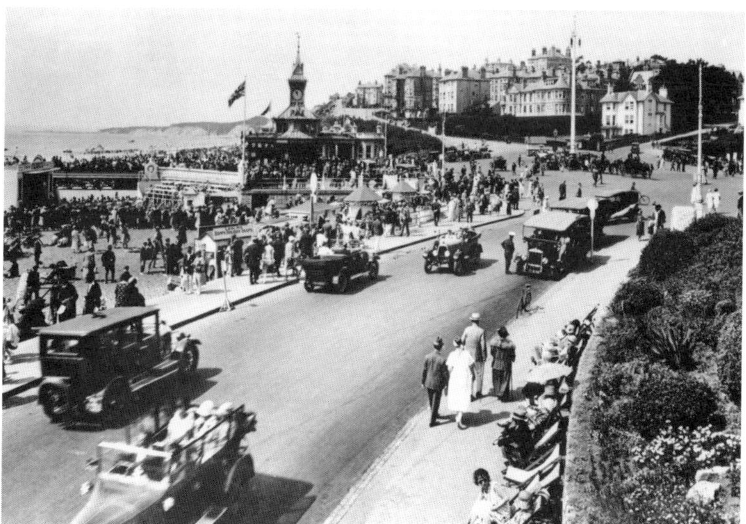

Boscombe developed to the east of Bournemouth in mid-Victorian times, attracting the wealthy and fashionable. Mineral springs added to Boscombe's attraction for those seeking an improvement to health, though it never became the spa it aspired to be.

BOSCOMBE

FROM THE PIER 1900 / 45232

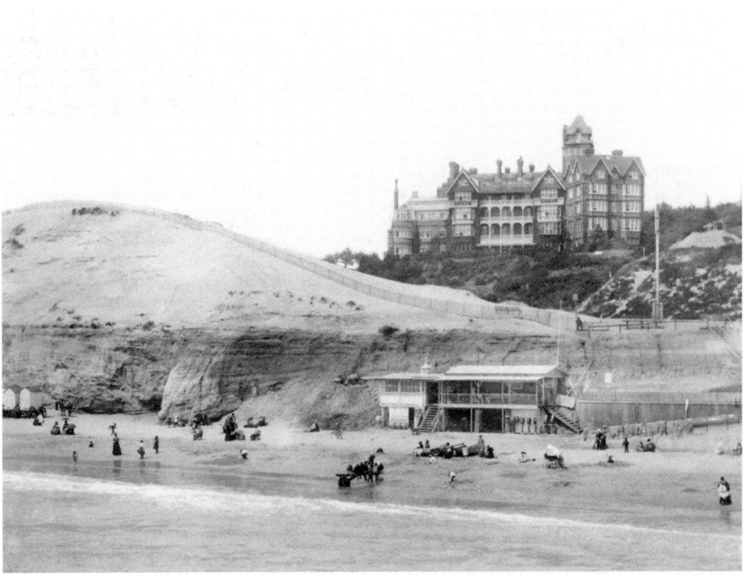

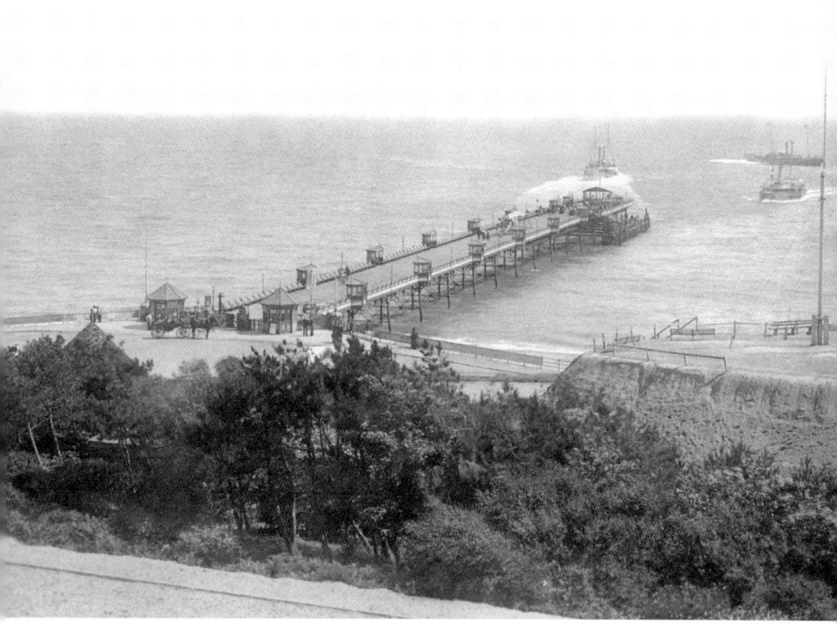

Like Bournemouth's pier, the structure at Boscombe was severely damaged in the Second World War, but both have been sympathetically restored. A third pier at Southbourne did not survive.

BOSCOMBE

THE PIER 1903 / 49156

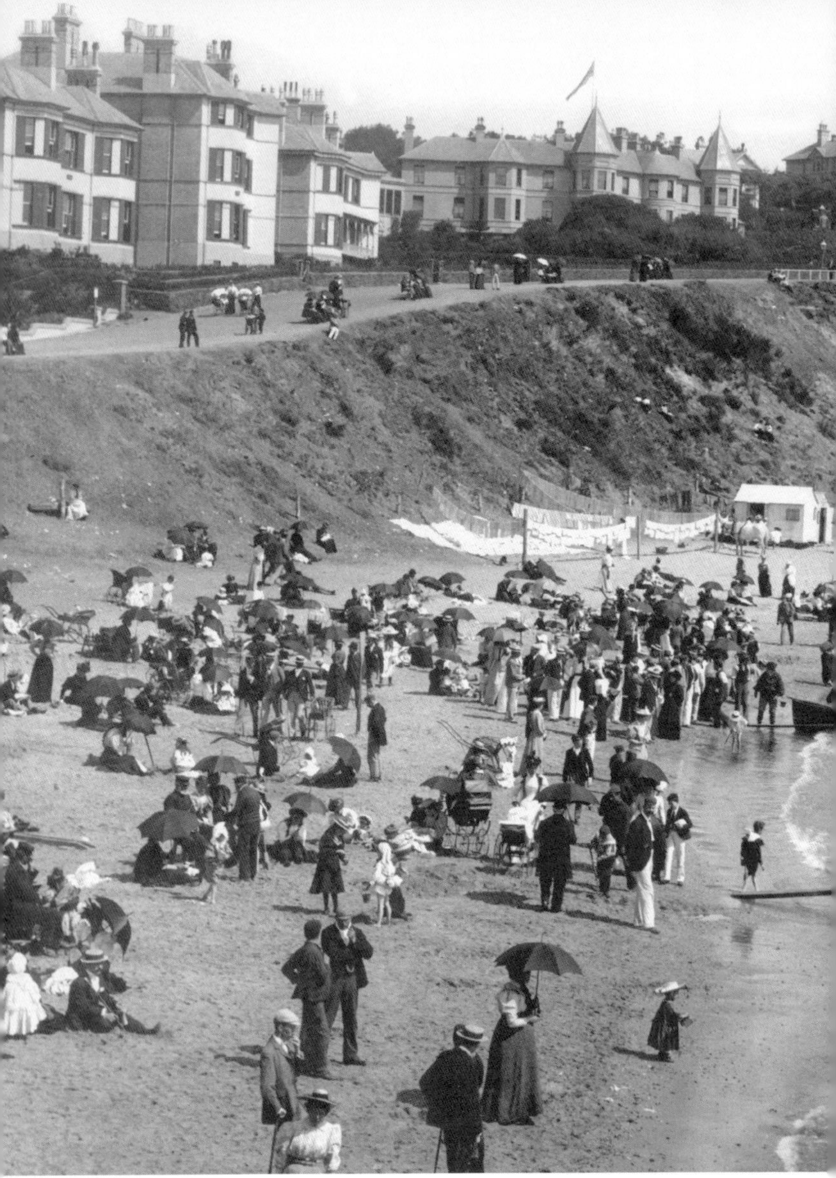

BOSCOMBE

FROM THE PIER 1903 / 49158

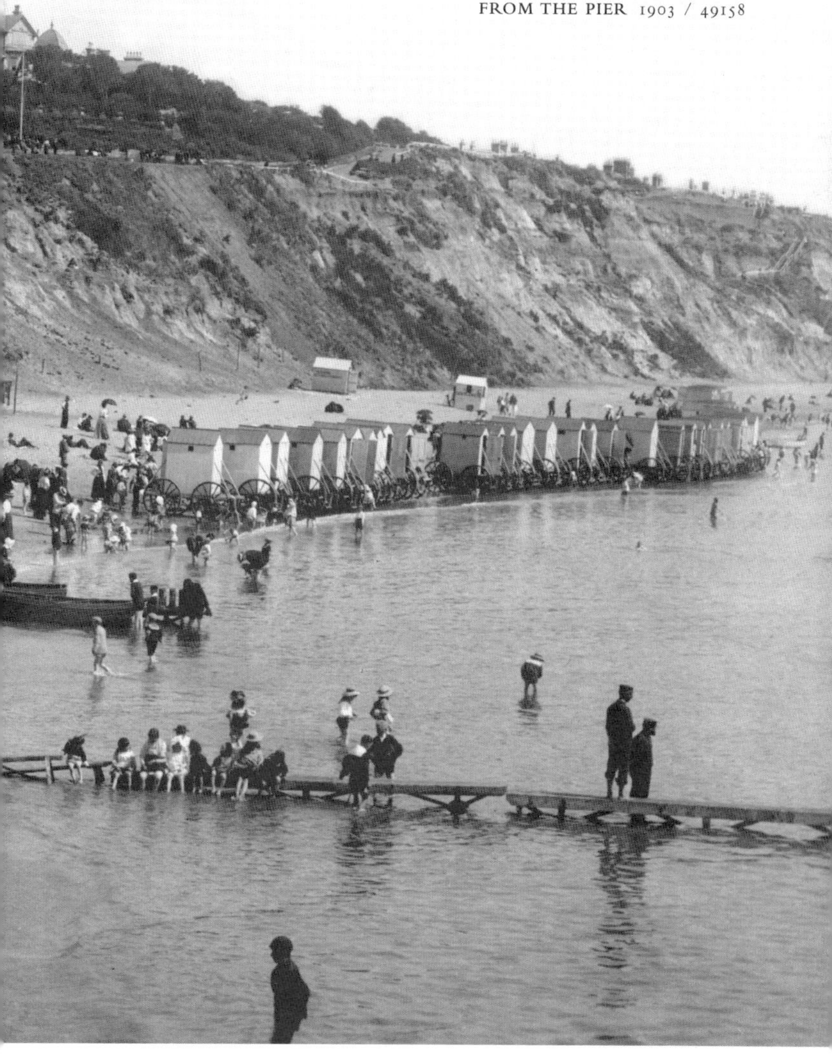

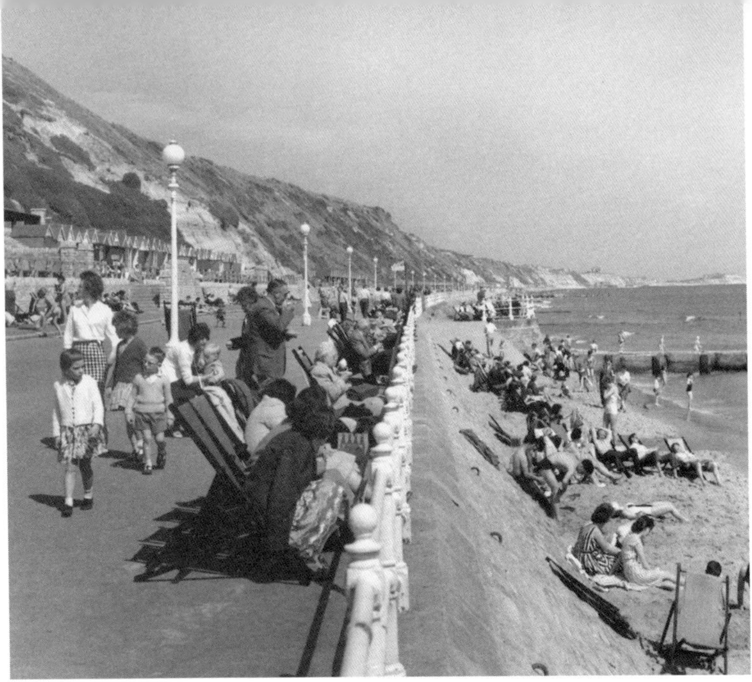

Southbourne stands above the seven miles of golden beaches that attract the tourist again and again to this part of the coast; a cliff railway facilitates access to the sands. By the 1950s, Southbourne had been almost completely swallowed up by the expanding Bournemouth district.

SOUTHBOURNE

THE PROMENADE c1955 / S153123

HIGHCLIFFE CASTLE

NEAR CHRISTCHURCH 1900 / 45059

Highcliffe Castle was once one of the grandest stately homes in southern England. Restoration is bringing it back to its former glory. The Grade I listed building was built by Lord Stuart de Rothesay in the Romantic style between 1830 and 1835; he employed the fashionable London architect William Donthorpe.

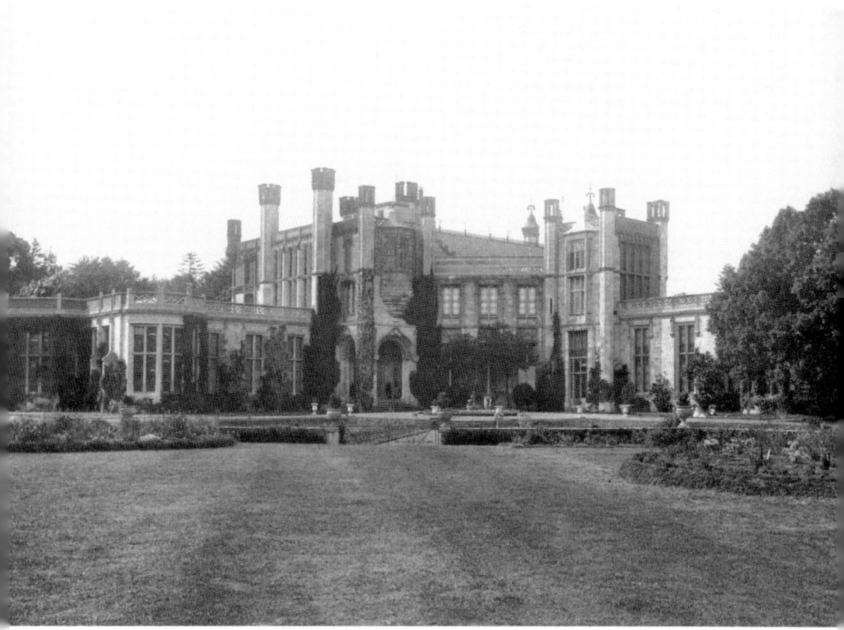

A peaceful scene at Wick Ferry, close to Christchurch. Even then, tourists were flocking to such picturesque places by foot, cycle, carriage and boat. This has developed into the massive crowds that flock nowadays into this area on hot summer days.

CHRISTCHURCH

WICK FERRY, THE WEST LANDING 1900 / 45045

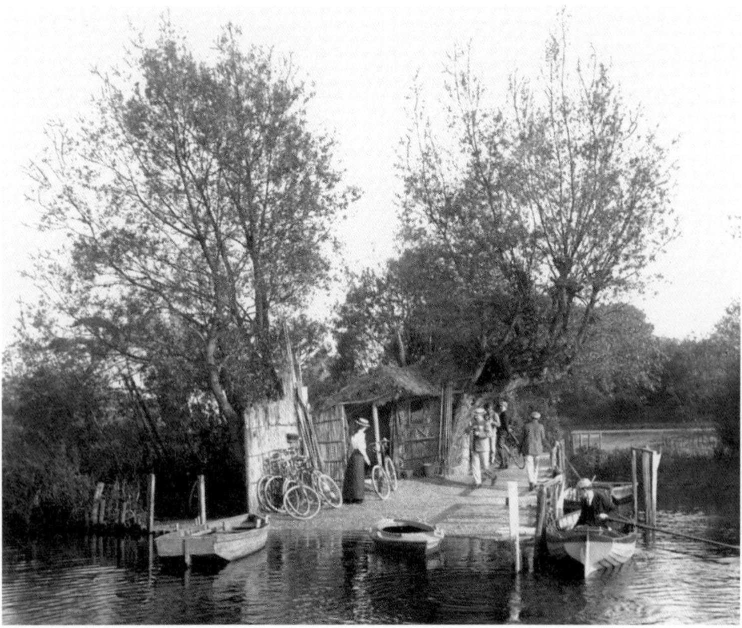

THOMAS HARDY'S DORSET VIEWS

Many of the places illustrated by the Frith family of photographers in Dorset would have been familiar to the poet and novelist Thomas Hardy. Hardy was born at Higher Bockhampton, near Stinsford, in 1840, working as an architect before achieving fame as a writer. In his famous Wessex series of novels, and in his poetry, he portrayed Dorset's countryside, towns and villages in detail, peopling them with the kind of country people he would have grown up with. Hardy left a fine legacy of novels, such as 'Far From the Madding Crowd', 'The Mayor of Casterbridge', 'The Trumpet-Major', 'Under the Greenwood Tree' and 'Tess of the D'Urbervilles', which are set firmly in a slightly-fictionalised Dorset landscape. As the 20th century dawned, Hardy abandoned novel writing in favour of poetry. He died at Max Gate, his home near Dorchester, in 1928.

It is possible to compare the Dorset portrayed by both Hardy and Frith by using the key below. On the left are Hardy's fictional Wessex place-names, on the right the geographical names as mentioned in this book.

Anglebury **Wareham**
Budmouth **Weymouth**
Casterbridge **Dorchester**
Chalk Newton **Maiden Newton**
Chaseborough **Cranborne**
Corvesgate Castle **Corfe Castle**
Emminster **Beaminster**
Evershead **Evershot**
Havenpool **Poole**
Isle of Slingers **Portland**
Knollsea **Swanage**
Little Hintock **Melbury Osmond**
Lulstead **Lulworth**
Nuzzleberry **Hazelbury Bryan**
Port Bredy **Bridport**
Sandbourne **Bournemouth**
Shaston **Shaftesbury**
Sherton Abbas **Sherborne**
Shottsford Forum **Blandford Forum**
Southerton **Wareham**
Tolchurch **Tolpuddle**
Weatherbury **Puddletown**

INDEX

Abbotsbury 80
Allington 29
Badbury Rings 28
Beaminster 31, 32, 33
Bindon Abbey 34
Blandford Forum 26–27
Boscombe 114, 115, 116–117
Bournemouth 109, 110–111, 112, 113
Bovington 35
Bridport 16–17
Brownsea Island 104
Burton Bradstock 76–77, 78
Canford 36
Charminster 37
Chideock 79
Christchurch 120
Corfe Castle 38, 39
Corfe Mullen 40
Cranborne 41
Dorchester 6, 8, 9, 10–11, 12, 13
Evershot 45
Frampton 42–43, 44
Frome Vauchurch 47
Godmanstone 46
Hazelbury Bryan 48
Highcliffe Castle 119
Higher Bockhampton 14–15
Hilton 49
Langton Matravers 50
Litton Cheney 51
Loders 52
Lulworth 94, 95, 96
Lyme Regis 68, 70–71, 72, 73, 74, 75
Maiden Newton 53, 54, 55
Melbury Osmond 56
Melplash 57, 58
Milton Abbas 59
Morcombelake 60
More Crichel 61
Moreton 62
Poole 105, 106, 107, 108
Portland 81, 82–83, 84
Puddletown 63, 64
Shaftesbury 18
Sherborne 19, 20, 21
Sixpenny Handley 65
Southbourne 118
Studland 102, 103
Swanage 97, 98–99, 100, 101
Tolpuddle 66
Wareham 22
Weymouth 85, 86–87, 88, 89, 90–91, 92–93
Wimborne 23, 24–25
Witchampton 67

PLEASE HELP US BRING FRITH'S PHOTOGRAPHS TO LIFE

Our authors do their best to recount the history of the places they write about. They give insights into how particular towns and villages developed, they describe the architecture of streets and buildings, and they discuss the lives of famous people who lived there. But however knowledgeable our authors are, the story they tell is necessarily incomplete.

Frith's photographs are so much more than plain historical documents. They are living proofs of the flow of human life down the generations. They show real people at real moments in history; and each of those people is the son or daughter of someone, the brother or sister, aunt or uncle, grandfather or grandmother of someone else. All of them lived, worked and played in the streets depicted in Frith's photographs.

We would be grateful if you would tell us about the many places shown in our photographs—the streets with their buildings, shops, businesses and industries. Describe your own memories of life in those streets: what it was like growing up there, who ran the local shop and what shopping was like years ago; if your workplace is shown tell us about your working day and what the building is used for now. With your help more and more Frith photographs can be brought to life, and vital memories preserved for posterity.

We will gradually add your comments and stories to the archive for the benefit of historians of the future. Wherever possible, we will try to include some of your comments in future editions of our books. Moreover, if you spot errors in dates, titles or other facts, please let us know, because our archive records are not always completely accurate—they rely on 150 years of human endeavour and hand-compiled records.

So please write, fax or email us with your stories and memories. Thank you!

FREE PRINT OF YOUR CHOICE

Choose any Frith photograph in this book.
Simply complete the Voucher opposite and return it with your remittance for £3.50 (to cover postage and handling) and we will print the photograph of your choice in SEPIA (size 11 x 8 inches) and supply it in a cream mount with a burgundy rule line (overall size 14 x 11 inches).

Please note: photographs with a reference number starting with a "Z" are not Frith photographs and cannot be supplied under this offer.
Offer valid for delivery to UK one address only.

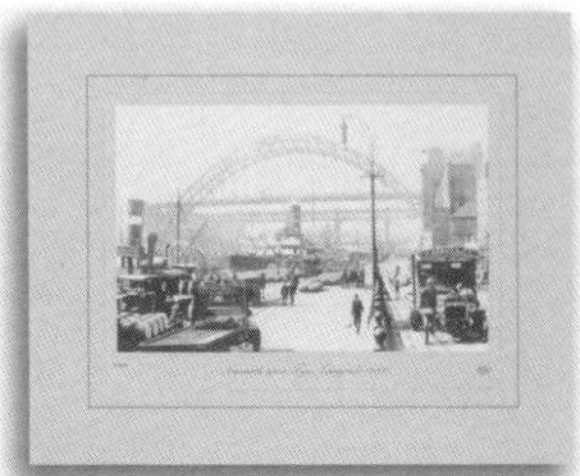

Mounted Print
Overall size 14 x 11 inches (355 x 280mm)

***PLUS:* Order additional Mounted Prints at HALF PRICE - £7.49 each** (normally £14.99)
If you would like to order more Frith prints from this book, possibly as gifts for friends and family, you can buy them at half price (with no additional postage and handling costs).

***PLUS:* Have your Mounted Prints framed**
For an extra £14.95 per print you can have your mounted print(s) framed in an elegant polished wood and gilt moulding, overall size 16 x 13 inches (no additional postage and handling required).

IMPORTANT!

These special prices are only available if you use this form to order. You must use the ORIGINAL VOUCHER (no copies permitted).

We can only despatch to one UK address. This offer cannot be combined with any other offer.

FRITH PRODUCTS AND SERVICES

All Frith photographs are available for you to buy as framed or mounted prints. From time to time, other illustrated items such as Address Books and Maps are also available. Already, almost 100,000 Frith archive photographs can be viewed and purchased on the internet through the Frith website.

For more detailed information on Frith companies and products, visit:

www.francisfrith.co.uk

For further information, or trade enquiries, contact:

The Francis Frith Collection, Frith's Barn, Teffont, Salisbury SP3 5QP

Tel: +44 (0) 1722 716 376 Fax: +44 (0) 1722 716 881 Email: sales@francisfrith.co.uk

Voucher *for FREE and Reduced Price Frith Prints*

Do not photocopy this voucher. Only the original is valid, so please fill it in, cut it out and return it to us with your order.

	Picture ref no	Page number	Qty	Mounted @ £7.49	Framed + £14.95	Orders Total £
1			1	**Free of charge***	£	£
2				£7.49	£	£
3				£7.49	£	£
4				£7.49	£	£
5				£7.49	£	£
6				£7.49	£	£
				* Post & handling		£3.50
				Total Order Cost		**£**

Please allow 28 days for delivery. Offer available to one UK address only

Title of this book . . . .

I enclose a cheque / postal order for £ . . . .
payable to 'The Francis Frith Collection'

OR debit my Mastercard / Visa / Maestro Card Number

Issue No (Maestro only) Valid from (Maestro)

Expires Signature

Name Mr/Mrs/Ms ....

Address ....

....

....

....Postcode...

Daytime Tel No ....

E-mail ....

ISBN: 1-84589-109-0 Valid to 31/12/08

Send completed Voucher form to:

The Francis Frith Collection, Frith's Barn, Teffont, Salisbury, Wiltshire SP3 5QP England

If you need more space, please write your address on a separate sheet of paper.